The Spring Branch

by Tony Shaffer

Sweetgum Press
Warrensburg, MO

The Spring Branch

Copyright ©2004 Tony Shaffer

ISBN 0-9728708-0-6

The Spring Branch was orignally published by UMI
Copyright ©1995 Tony Shaffer

Cover and chapter art concepts
by Tony Shaffer

Sweetgum Press
Warrensburg, Missouri

Dedicated to my son, Alex,
in the hope that
the cycles continue
in him

January

January 1

Does it mean something?

Who is the man who stands by the river?
– casting a line
– catching or not
– watching the flow
– taking it in
– searching for . . .
– learning . . .
– understanding.

What is this thing?
Is it worth doing?
Will it lead to an answer?
Does it have meaning?
Is it good?
Why do it?

Twixt the poet and the fisherman,
the difference is nil;
The poet fills his cache,
while the fisherman catches his fill.

This is the beginning – of the linear cycle.
The phases of the moon and the stages of the man
Lunar life cycles – development
The first day of the new year offers promise of new things;
But the thing is the thing –
Isn't it?

Life is like . . .
Well . . .
Life.

Isn't it?

To the seeker the cycle is new again.
To the learner the answers are the same again.
To the fisherman life is the key.
To the poet, the key is life . . .

All, all in a cycle of renewal and progression – never
changing, ever new.
      Doing.

January 2

Already, the sense of time impinges upon the enjoyment of
   the moment.
The passage of time makes itself known
      in the ticking of the clock
      in the marking of the calendar
      in the remembrance of writing the new date
        on a check
      in the lengthening of the day
      and of the "new" times
        for sunset and sunrise

It is time
      to take the tackle from the shelf
      to mend last year's apparent wear
      to put the knife to the whetstone
      to catalogue the missing elements
      to sort and repair and prepare
      to draw the worn books from the shelf
and to read the words of those writers
   who SAW and KNEW and DID

           and to reflect –

What matters rhyme if the poet could poeticize?
   the rhythm is the thing
     the words is the thing
       the word is the thing

the thing is the thing

I have my favorite poets:
McClane, Schwiebert, Lyons, Bergman,
Traver, Raymond, Slaymaker,
    and the Circle (may he be unbroken)
    and one of the Waltons, but not John-boy.

January 3

THE OPENING SCENE (framed):
    A boy walks down a country lane, frozen in the moment. Trees line both sides of the lane and the boy takes long barefooted strides toward a creek visible in the distance. His mouth puckers in a whistle. A cane pole rests on his shoulder, line wrapped around it and tied to a bent pin. His red shirt and faded overalls denote his life's station but belie his majesty – a prince and a pauper. A ripped straw hat sags over his eyes but allows one curly lock to drape his collar. The Prince Albert can (better let him out) in his hip pocket is opened and the nightcrawlers are trying to escape a fate unknown and unforeseen, but somehow dreaded. It is likely that the boy intends to catch bluegill or catfish in the creek. Or maybe, perchance, a carp or sucker or drum or eel will seek him out. That doesn't matter – what does matter is that the boy knows the thing even though he doesn't know he knows it.

HE is the first word of the poem.

    but who is he?
Call me Huck Finn.
    (but Huck Finn died, no he lives in books,
        but they are banned –
    I thought there was just one,
        no he lives in all of them)
    Hemingway knew that
        and how to land a trout.

January 4

SCENE 2:

Me & Izaak went fishing. (the editors don't like this, they would rather I not use the cliche, but they don't realize that the simple can still be the true; and the vices versa. and they would rather I write than go fishing – "give a boy a fishing pole or a banjo or a fiddle or let him be some kind of writer or poet or lawyer, and you might as well give him a ticket straight to HELL!" Sooo...)

Me & Izaak went fishing. We left catching to those who needed to do that and concentrated on our mission. Izaak was there to teach and Me was there to learn. We had some adventures and writ them down. Lord knows we had trials, but we maintained.

And the following dialogue is absolutely unimportant, so it is included, thusly:

ANGLATOR: grocerystor!
SPORTSTOR: applecor!
METAPHOR: Baltimor!
– Who's your friend?
– WE!

ANGLATOR: Do you understand the importance the meaning the purpose of it?
SPORTSTOR: Yes well maybe well not really well no not at all
ANGLATOR: Very well, then. First we may concentrate on your technique and presentation. Do you have a graphite rod and multi-polymer line?
SPORTSTOR: Yes here is one and the other is yet blank
ANGLATOR: No, that is a pencil and will not serve our purpose yet.
When casting a line, use a medium-weight outfit suited to the waters.

>   Be sure it balances and will not overload
>   and startle the quarry.
>   Observe detail and employ
>   a proper tapered leader.
>   Notice that in God's plan,
>   even a fly is significant.
>   Be on the waters before the light of day has
>   clarified and simplified.
>   Master a simple cast and ensure that
>   the hook at the end of the line is not
>   bent or broken or rusty.

SPORTSTOR: Slow down you go too fast I can't keep up it's too much.
METAPHOR: Sounds like work to me.
ANGLATOR: IS work, you mean. You lack self-awareness, Metaphor.
Now – do it.
SPORTSTOR: You mean learn by doing?
ANGLATOR: Naa! DO by learning.
SPORTSTOR: Is this a test?
ANGLATOR: imonial.
SPORTSTOR: Then I'm itchen for it, laddy!
METAPHOR: So this THING is like the other THING, right?
ANGLATOR: IS! IS! IS! Keep up, Metaphor!

January 5

See the waters
    the reflective surface offers clues and hints to the
        mysteries below
    sunlight danses alongside the mayfly
    when the sunbeams angle just so, then
    the depths are revealed
    the revolution of evolution shows in microcosm in the
        spring branch
    the creatures crawl swim fly walk to complete the cycle
    and the wealth of the waters is fecundity

and the beauty of the waters is hypnotic
and the movement of the waters sustains and purifies
as the spring feeds the branch.

Hear the waters
as the branch flows over boulders and pebbles and falls
and the gurgle gurgle oxygenates and sweeps the debris
and the wind blows the branches of the trees
and creates riffles in the surfaces of the pools
and birds chirrup the spirit
and crickets and frogs announce attendance
at the danse of the waters

Feel the waters
as the current pushes against submerged limbs
as the icy cold spring water draws the heat from the
  body
as the cold wetness belies the lifegiving qualities
hidden in the atoms and molecules of the earth in
  microcosm
as the waters meet the shores

Smell the waters
carrying the riches and richness of the earth
the scent of last autumn's leaves
the mint of spring along the fertile bank
the myriad of wildflowers popping up like weeds
and the fishy smell of promised rewards

Taste the waters
and the purity of the earth
and notice the cold wet sweetness
taste of the wild and of the free
let it be part of you
as you are a part of it
taste of life
and sense the wonder of it

January 6

METAPHOR: So are you saying that fishing is like life or that life is like the long poem or that fishing is like the long poem or that life is like fishing?
                          Or what?
ANGLATOR: Oh, go dig worms.

SPORTSTOR: You mean that it's all right to use worms?
ANGLATOR: Listen – here's the THING:

A bait fisherman just doesn't know
       doesn't know what
about the ritual
       what ritual
the ritual of fishing
       but does he catch trout
only the dumb ones
       but does he know the river
only down deep
       but is a bait a lure

no, my only hope for salvation
is the possibility that this fish knows
the purposes of fishing
and cooperates
otherwise . . . it's all the same.

January 7

        And so the poem?
            YES!

In this day of this month of the year of our Lord . . .
The cycle continues.
       Whether uni-, bi-, tri-, or motor-,
This "long poem" business just tries to express
       "another way of looking"

when seeing is what matters.

The poets seek . . . what – but find it not.
        answers are for fools
        destinations are for the lost
the only hope is to know and do
the only right road is the one being traveled
the only worthy purpose is to try
and the only goal is TO BE
anything else is trivial
and only for style
but needs to
be done
if only
to

Give Purpose and Meaning to the Quest for Understanding by Putting Form into Life, that is, to put Life into Form, and to somehow Try to Communicate a Level of Truth (however relative) to any Seeker by Finding the Universe in the Microcosm and Portraying It in Symbols, whether Letters, Words, Sentences, Lines, Prose, Poetry, Prosody, Proetry, or Pose.

Think about the trivial and think about the long poem and think and think and think.

Is the best answer TRUTH or is it just the best answer?
        And what, if anything, is truly trivial?

(which reminds me – I missed you last night; did you just forget . . . or not care?)

January 8

(on this day a king was born?)

The king of the wandering peoples was born this day,
but the legends omit the telling of the birth of his twin brother.
What if . . .
The True King was the one died in childbirth?
Or if both souls entered the one who lived?
Or if the signs were wrong and this one –
was not the true king?

                The Sign of Authenticity
was found by an archaeologist who
wandered out of the southern desert
through the foothills of Sierra Madre
babbling and raving
holding the quest object reverently, saying:

"Behold the painting of El Vis
The Neon Flouresced color of his likeness
The blackness of his background
(real velveteen)
But look at the EYES –
and walk with me . . .
See how they seem to follow you around the room?"
And none could doubt the correctness of his vision
And the loyal made the pilgrimage
Down the river
Past Cairo to Memphis
Seeking the land of Grace

Believing that they knew
Keeping the flame alive
Even beyond his earthly death
His essence remains . . .
                Thank you . . . thank you very much!

January 9

and so –

just what is the significance of a long poem
        that doesn't rhyme (but does roam)
        that may not cohere
        that few will go near
        that is green and not orange
        that . . . that . . . that . . .

is about fishing???

but then again, what isn't it about?

the cycle contains all and all contain cycles
        how many wheels?
bi-'s tri-'s uni-'s and motor-'s
wheels within wheels spinning backwards
fabricating a rubric of relative significance
between the bookends of "rant" and "rave"
that cannot be known except by doing
whatever
but by DOing it RIGHT!

But then –
this is an INSTRUCTUAL manual rather than an
INSTRUCTIONAL manual
a manual
        of labor, hence of birth, hence daysed by birth into a
        daze, like dace.

may the cycle be unbroken
        in this guy lord in this guy . . .

January 10

listen:
This "Long Pome Business" is full of corporate raiders and
    samurai accountants
who look at a poem and say "what's in it for me?"
reading the Donne & Bradstreet report
and trying to find something to take stock in
it's like buying something they'll never see
and trying to sell it at a profit
oh, sure – futures are holding steady
pork bellies are on the rise
liberated women are shaving their legs
the war is over so what the hell
a true meeting of minds or trivialities
can be found in
the long rod and the long poem
(it's not how long it is it's how well it casts)

and
note the arc created by moving through the casting cycle:
    10:00 2:00 10:00 2:00
shoot the line   double haul
roll (like a wheel)   get the timing right
make a gentle presentation to the lie

(the lie=a disruption in the current in which sustenance can
    be gathered with impunity)

and in the lie, the WISE (relatively speaking) old trout lurks
    in the riffle
picking off drifting nymphs and slurping with hooked
    mandible
rising to the danse of the mayflies upon the waters
and carrying out his part of the cycle within the cycle
    as the poets exist within the food chain
and learn to eat or be eaten
and learn, like the trout, to see always without eyelids

January 11

Ranchero Quervo

To Whom It May Concern:

Know that the fisherpoet, being in full possession of his faculties, has endeavored to display the DEPTH of MEANING of his
PURSUITS.

At no time will the poet attempt to fool any other than the trout who inhabit the spring branch and who, if there is justice in the world, are aware of the deceit and recognize the concommittance of the goals underlying
                the art of angling

or, in particular, of using the long rod as a THING in itself,
        not to be confused with
                the avocation of fishing.

As this does seem to come under the heading of BUSINESS, then let all concerned be aware that a life's work can be adjudged MEANINGFUL without UNDERSTANDING if the mere trait of RESPECT is applied, (by fysshe, pome, angeler, and poitzer), noting that the NAME is not the THING which is, in actuality, the same in each and every case. Nor is it in this book or in any other book – it resides within only and solely the propriety of the readership, and not the writership, although the writer can pier beyond the veil of superficiality.
        to be remembered: it all pays the same.

yrs trly
the fisherpoet (never to be construed or confused as being
        related to the anglophile –
or other independent contractor borrowing from the
        architecture of LORE)

January 12

So who will buy this book?
Poets? or Fishermen?

Uh-oh
i can hear it now –
what is this stuff about fisherMAN
how about fisherperson
these are times of equality
ok then what do we do with a fisherking?
depose him?
or desex him? –
it's too late – he's wounded and martyred
like Jesus
Christ was a fisher
wasn't that enough
altho casting a fly is easier than casting bread,
    (both get soggy, but "Fly-Dry" works;
        bread gives up the ghost)

and then there's that guy in oklahoma who never met a man
        he didn't like
how did he feel about women
or politicians
i guess he was right even tho he may not have been correct

yes, but,
so then –
who will buy this book?
poets?
no.
they would only buy this book to review for a journal and
even in that case they would really just be trying to get a
little extra bread or looking for stuff to steal
(they already know the thing, but they always need more
        STUFF)
better they should go fish for it.

alrightalready –
WHO, then?

Just: you.

January 13

and maybe friends and relatives
and maybe some guys
(operating definition; GUYS: people, persons, human beings
    of any gender;
sexism will not be tolerated, but then neither will
intolerance.
just note that "he" is not the same as "He" and that
SOMEBODY took away all my pronouns . . .
I can't use you, even tho "I" can use "you"
and "you" can use "me"
so, hopefully, (op.def.: full of hope) the first person who
    reads this book
will tell the second person to read this book
and that person (you) will tell a third person to read this
book
and maybe number and gender will not be as important as
    once was thought

but will this ever be in the cannon?
no.
a bunch of guys should be in the cannon
ram them home with wadding behind them
and then touch off the powder
listen to the roar
watch the trajectory
see where they land
and how much damage they can cause
take no prisoners
praise the lord and praise the ammunition
pass them beans

I learnt to write from a bunch of guys
        Twain and Crane and Crane
        Whitman and Emerson and Hemingway
        London McGuane and Ellison (HnotR)
        Fitzgerald Pound Poe Faulkner
        Lardner Bierce Vonnegut
        Ruark Pynchon Updike
        Percy Mathiessen Roth
        Salinger Melville
and last
        Zukofsky
        – one who could cast a line
        and knew the lure
        I'd love to fish with him
        but I wonder if he ever caught a trout . . .

January 14

but, wait a minute . . .
be rationale
this structure, this LACK of structure is not like any poem
        of worth
there is no rhyme rhythm meter et cetera
why its some sort of blank verse

no.

blank verse is an oxymoron

this is my idea of blank verse:

_____
    _____
   _____
     _____
  _____
      _____
 _____
    _____
_____

Notice line length – that everyother line is indentated
Notice that with each line the idea is inundated
Notice that each idea is contemporarily dated
Notice that each sound is similarly related
Notice the rhyme scheme is A,A,A,A-ted
huh – sure sounds addlepated.

sure, but i'd rather cast metaphors than morphemes
metallurgy is less significant than morpheus
no man is an ireland
but that was in another river, and all the fish were dead

January 15

then what caliber of poet wrote this?

a more powerful poet at .44 than at .38
more accurate at .38 than at .22
not as scattered as 20 ga. or even
especially at 12 ga.
on target
loaded

primed
measuring muzzle velocity
sighting with a scope
checking the bore
adjusting the sights
keeping the powder dry
aiming at one quail rather than at the covey
cleaned and oiled
tracking the game
enjoying the feel of the stock
observing the rules of safety
not going off half-cocked
identifying the target
sighting carefully
squeezing the trigger
holding the breath
and . . . squeezing, not pulling
and watching the puff of smoke
and knowing before the firing that the quarry will be struck

but always, always being a true sportsman and gentleman
(substitute "person" or whatever yer little heart desires)

not like Billy the Kid, resting near Tombstone on the Avon
or that gunslinger out in colorado
who made a name for himself
by gunning down the
names of yore

lordy, he was fast.

January 16

and so –

it is cold and snowy blowy here at the cabin and the fever rages. there is time – time to pull the books from the shelves and peruse the anecdotes of reflective fisherpoets. their thoughts bring back memories of other days on other streams but this only feeds the fever, the cold remains starved. and so – the worn leatherbound volumes offer little solace to one who needs to DO rather than reflect. the wind howls and moves the snow in minor and major patterns that would be quite obvious, if the seer had but a higher perspective. the fire wanes but the fever rages and the red setter curls by the fireplace dreaming dog dreams of running and casting for scent. the books lead to cataloging the memories. *a day on the yellowstone when the browns suicidally attacked hoppers. a day on the beaver dams when brookies inhaled streamers. a day floating on a North Dakota pond when rainbows devoured woolybuggers twitched deep. a day on the spring branch when the big one nailed an Adams and leapt several times higher than its length and wore itself out in a beautiful albeit ineffectual struggle.* the memories lead to cataloging the tackle. *the waders still leak. the hat still slouches. the vest still protrudes in unnatural places dutifully lugging all manner of necessary minutiae. things need to be oiled. flies need to be steamed to straighten the hackles and to unbefoul the marabou. each pocket of the vest releases its collection of temporarly gathered stuff never removed. each pocket is a mystery with clues to yet another story. and many contain fly boxes housing little soldiers organized by rank and size into little armies prepared to mount a sortie on stream life, to infiltrate subjugate and otherwise fool one of god's innocent creatures into believing that something that looks good enough to be real can be good enough to eat.* after the flies are sorted, terminal tackle is inventoried. *lead in different quantities takes the lure deep. leaders taper meaningfully. lines must be oiled. the long rod must be waxed and the guides polished individually. hooks need to be filed hollow pointedly and checked for rust. the reel requires dis- and re-assembly and cleaning and lubricating. drag washers show wear, but are still ok. leather wants oil whether on a creel or in a reel. finally it all goes back to its shelf to wait to wait and to fuel the reflections.* and the setter sleeps snoringly.

and the fire crackles warmingly. and the tackle rests impatiently. and – all the chores done – the poet writes. in longhand on a legal pad or in the English leather binder or in the neglected entries to the fishing journal or on a Sierra card to another fisherpoet or to all those who have not been writ to in a long while. and the memories cue other memories and the train spirals backwards to new hopes and regretted missed chances. and the bourbon swirls mistily about the ice and the head nods and the hands come to rest and the soul joins that of the red setter, running and casting.

January 17

under the ice, life stirs
the spring branch feeds the cycle
and keeps passages open
for all god's critters who just want to live and procreate
and fruitfully fulfill their own cycles

the metabolism slows
the requirements are less
but Trout, Unlimited sees to it that they are met
the damning of the spring branch will not be permitted
weirs can help to keep the waters open

but, even if the property is owned –
(did the same god who gave kings divine rights
also invent ownership of lands and waters?)
water rights (same god again?) disallow misuse
of the resources.

life finds a way
and if there is no way
there is no life

under the surface, the mystery,
veiled though it may be,
wends its way through the cycles

helped or hindered by
well-meaning peoples

who have only recently
come to understand:

what it means.

January 18

and it comes to the surface
and it is pome-like in form
altho the form be part of
if not the THING

is there a recipe for the form?
well, hardly
i mean
there are recipes for an Adams
        and for trout almondine
        and for love potion #9
        and for aunt martha's extra-special strudel

but

what about this THING?

i mean

where would it start what would it contain what are the rules
        who decides
what does it look like what is right or wrong
how long should it be how does it end
?

ok . . .

        ok –

its not just the lines – that would make it a highway
its not just rhyme – cos thats not there all the time
its not just words – or it would be a dictionary
its not just meter – or it would be non-free-parking
its not just the elements – altho they do form everything
as do poets, and make up matter – as the poet makes up
        what matters
its not –

a lotion or a potion or the motion of the ocean or
        devotion to a notion land-o-goshen

its what it is
and if it portrays the THING then it may be a text
whatever that is
and it defines itself anew as it goes along
and these particles must be in the thing in whatever amounts
        are proscribed
without prescription

January 19

well, surely it contains symbols – right?
        sure
and they are identifiable – right?
        sure
and they follow traditional symbolism – right?
        su-...hold it! let's just do this right now
        so that we can get past it

air	=	winter
earth	=	fall
water	=	spring
fire	=	summer

now throw that out
and look for what is really there to find

as far as i am concerned, the four humours are
                      good
                      bad
                      indifferent
                      and parody

but i want parity
so take note:

the thing is the thing
the THING is the THING!

even if it is obsession
(do you understand obsession?)
with the mundane
and with the trivial

because how can you tell which is which
        without a scorecard?
and i gave mine away
to someone who seemed to need one

because i dont keep score when its happening
and only when i look back
can i see that all those winding roads
form a straight line

and when you look back you can see
you either got it or you didn't

January 20

but if you truly need some sort of recipe
if you truly need some sort of symbol
if you need something to hold it all together
then i will do that for you
why?
because i like you

kae-ee-why

it is a pot of soup
yes
and it cooks on a back burner
constantly simmering
always ready to give sustenance
needing occasionally to be stirred
and sometimes revealing what makes its substance
and i taste it as it simmers
occasionally adding a dash of this or that
and once in a while putting in a pinch of spice
as it needs
but following no plan
not pouring from a can
not even using a soup-starter kit
just starting from scratch
and thinking about what i liked in the soups of others
and wanting to incorporate but still to originate
and wanting to make it rich enough
for any who might drop by
if they have the hunger

do i need to tell you more?

i would rather you just take it as it is
because without a recipe
i will never make this particular broth again

huh? oh . . . ok
air	=	boiling bubbles
water	=	broth
earth	=	meat and vegetables
fire	=	the stove

the proportions (putting enough STUFF into the soup)
depend on either the hoodooing
                       or the whodoing . . .

January 21

there are choices to make
why the long rod
is it better more efficient a bigger challenge
personally meaningful superior in some way
        no
            not intrinsically
it is like a religion
and one that works for me might not work for you
it gives meaning and values form
and, at times, displays all those characteristics
but, hopefully, not in a snobbish way
i would not deign to lose sight of humble beginnings
and my ultimate goal is to be
in the log cabin
where i can be reborn
which is where abe lincoln started
which is to say that there was a simple joy
in those humble beginnings and a jaded spirit can find
purpose in regaining that, somehow, again
remember when . . .
the world was a big exciting place
        containing myriads of things and experiences
        all new
        all full of possibility
        and with choices galore
        and the need to DO

well, maybe that's what the long rod
        or the long pome
                DO

just offer a chance at simple joy and another perspective on
the worldly world
and just possibly
give a respite
however brief

so that we can go on
with that one thing
the gift that is so hard to come by
and yet so simple:

                     hope

January 22

do i deconstruct myself?
very well then, i deconstruct myself

i am a nineties guy, but too late to be raised
       from a yuppy puppy
a lackey to the dream in the eighties who woke up
a wanderer in the seventies who came home
a child of the sixties who grew up
and a baby of the boom who had the advantages
       and numbers

in light of all this
i or my text is a construct
and my language reflects that
somewhat

and my attitudes came from my environs which were
middle west
middle class
which is ok
i had to start somewhere

being in the middle lets me be
liberal but not left
conservative but not right
and suggests balance

it also allows me change in any direction
because i am starting from the center
so

if you deconstruct my text or me
from any perspective or slant
you should qualify yourself

because i may not be what i appear
at any time because that may be what i was then
because i too am in a cycle
and i too seek progression

and if you chop away some of my words to find meaning
you chop at me too
save yourself some time
and me some grief

January 23

this is just a pome
not even a rime, as such
and it makes no claims other than
as greetings to fellow travelers
who find themselves wondering along a path
seeking something
and who have heard it suggested that
what they seek is rather trivial
all things considered
after all
if beauty is individually perceived
so is triviality
if it is my time
let me spend it as i will
if it is my love
let me share it with those
whom i love
and who love me
and on those things
giving meaning to my life
and, if i so choose, on a pome
or even   fishing

January 24

two friends of mine were poets
or writers in spirit
but they could not find the time to rite
they had IMPORTANT STUFF to do
and RESPONSIBILITIES
and families
and children
and jobs
and goals
and so they didn't apply pen to paper
they planned on doing that sort of thing
when the golden years of retirement afforded time
and so they worked through their dayse
occasionally giving glimpses of the visions
that they possessed and of the manner
in which they would one day write them down
and they were unique, sensitive, beautiful, wonderful
and fleeting
and gone now forever because they were never written
too many interruptions
too much stress
too much of a lifestyle proscribed by the times
one departed this life never having written more than a page
never having reached the golden years
just sort of wearing down early and stopping too soon
the other did reach retirement
but was too tired
or distracted
to write
so those dreams went with them
some would say that the important thing is to have dreamed
    at all
or that life itself is the poem they each wrote
that is true if that was the intention
but i consider it a responsibility to SHARE
rather than give

January 25

and so . . .
this pome.

about, of all things, fishing
and fly-fishing at that.
is this a way for a grown man to spend his time?
it will not change the world
or end war
or feed the hungry
or shelter the homeless
it will not make me rich
(however, discern between that and wealthy)
and it will not ingratiate me with those
who feel that these are idle pursuits
for malingerers and ne'erdowells
from their perspectives

so what good is it
anyway

well . . .
as the tidal wave begins with the first ripple
and as the tornado begins with the first breeze
       arising from the stillness
consider the possibility
that larger things may grow
in directions not originally perceived
if you would take a day and spend it fishing
in a spring branch
not necessarily catching, altho that would be ok
you might just learn something
or feel something
and tho you might not find the time energy and money there
       to change the world
you might find the inertia, overcome entropy,
and find yourself a state of mind

or of grace
and be able to carry that to other facets of your world
and influence a little change
in your corner of it
and . . .

January 26

so this is it.
the idle pursuit of the longrodpome
on the hierarchy of avocation
each represents the epitome of form superseding practicality
to a point of no longer being purposeful
at least in the view of an outsider
or one who has not learned to look in and appreciate

if i tried to teach you to fish
i would fail
if i tried to get you to listen to this pome
i would fail

because you will come to these
when you are seeking
because all paths lead to water
eventually
and all streams lead to the sea

and the trick is to stop for a moment and look
and wonder where the stream goes
but more importantly
where it comes from
turn and look back

follow against the current
toward the eternal and take the
upstream path
to its source
and eventually

you will come to the
spring branch

January 27

preparations begin likewise for many things
commotion disruption in the ordinary
confusion in what is necessary
it is hard to discard what is only convenient
and to pare down to what is essential

but it must be done because poets
like fisherpersons and campers
are gadgeteers
and collect all manner of little devices
which seem, upon obtaining,
to serve a most needful purpose
and only upon embarkation
turn into extra weight
sometimes these are carried fully up the mountain
and then there is no way to get rid of them
it would be littering to throw them away
not to mention desecration of a special place
and they rob the fisherpoet of the
      beauty of simplicity
and of travelling light

i try to choose well what i will carry
and bring only what will serve
a fisherpoet
and enhance being
the rod the pencil the vest the boots
and of course the hat
and i mottoize myself
– when in doubt leave it out –
but i do not restrict myself either
and after i determine what i really need
i try to carry as much as i can

because there is always the unforeseen
to deal with

January 28

do you have a good knife?
surely you know it is the most indispensable survival tool
and that it more than makes up for its weight
choose yourself whether form supersedes function
but be reasonable
i have seen men stride creeks with a bowie harnessed on
and others waltz into the bank with a folding buck strapped
        to a belt
still others carry silver penknives, monogrammed and flimsy
these would be all right, i guess
if one wanted to cut down a tree or cut costs or trim a cigar
        or core an apple
all worthwhile pursuits in their places but . . .
i carry one that is good and sturdy
functional
artistic in its simplicity
old and worn
resharpened many times
dulled in color at the blade and the grip
from years of heavy use
it won't down an oak
but it will whittle a toothpick
or cut a line
or clean a trout
and it travels well
it folds
and goes into a pocket
pants when walking vest when fishing
and it has been lost more than once
but it has been found
i was told to choose well . . .
that there would be a time when it mattered.

January 29

do you carry pencils
or pens
or a word processor
or herr-portable doktor smith-corona
or how about that new gadget the portable laptop
how wondrous
or do you
like i
have a place wherein all these things reside
in spirit if not in body
and where you go when you need to write
a good place is all you need
and perhaps you don't need to be writing when
       you are not there
oh, sometimes it is nice to write at a spot
i once sat on the stoop of a guesthouse in Bath
and wrote several short poems and letters
(because missives serve the same master and purpose,
       you know)
and needed to write there
if at all
so it was nice to have a good pencil and a clean legal pad
for those times when i could not get to the writing place
and did need to write it down
so that i would not forget it
but, mostly
when i am out
i am collecting sorting arranging thinking doing being
and taking what i find back with me
to the writing place
and then
putting it together.

January 30

do you have a vest
or waders or boots
or a good fly rod
or a hat
I have worn many hats and boots
and the only difference is who i am at the time
my hat, like my other possessions
was chosen when needed
and worn whenever
other hats have temporarily been worn
because i did not realize that i already had the right one
and so this one is old weatherbeaten faded slouchy
    almost shapeless
and suits me, keeping rain and sun from my eyes
my boots, however, have often been worn
    past the point of repair
and have required replacement
which means breaking them in
it is always wise to have an extra pair
just in case

regarding fly rods, tho, i probably have too many
one my height for small streams
another much longer for rivers
one that looked good at the store
another that is perfect for a middle-sized stream
one almost weightless for windless days
another that i built myself
one given to me by a friend
another that i inherited

but all these offer variety in approach
and oftentimes that is what is most needed
no method will work in all circumstances
and being locked in obliterates versatility
so i allow myself choices in this matter

and i think where i am going
and what the weather is like
and what the water is like
and what it is I want to DO
when i get there.

January 31

the ritual's the thing
and whether it be a bloodsport or a religion
serves to give awareness to the cycles
and rhythms of life

wanton destruction is not the point;
catching is not always the point
just being and doing can suffice
and the ritual of the long rod/pome
and of the fisherpoet
find identity in the seeker
of life

and just as a child who has never killed
can play games of death
with relish
so the fisherpoet
who has drawn blood
who has cleaned and cooked game
in the ritual
has an appreciation for all life
and an abhorrence of unnecessary death

through ritual and form
craft becomes artistry
ritual becomes essence
form becomes meaning

in-and-of-itself

February

February 1

How cold it is –
the only warmth available is from external embers
in the fireplace or in the bourbon
or when the red setter curls at my feet

my soul is at low ebb
my spark at its weakest
but in the cold dark
there is a glimmer emanating from a scintilla of an idea
that the cycle is coming around
and that when this page is torn from the calendar
the season will be open

the coming weeks will mark the slow awakening
       of enthusiasm
and a renewed sense of purpose
as events lead toward newend beginnings
even in the face of snow wind ice

over the years
the month has served to belie its shortness
and seeming lack of significance
transposition of this period
from time-out to time-in
as given new reason to savor this
as all moments should be savored

once an occasion for misfortunes
now miracles abound

celebration

February 2

It is time to call upon old friends

i pass the hours
making the best use of this seeming pause
and do what i can
to connect once again
with those who will be going with me

i start with McClane
and take him from my bookshelf
he tells me about
  practicalities
  poetics
  balance
and solving problems

and he tells me
what i already knew
but needed to hear again
in order to prepare

and he tells me about this . . .
trout
as do others
whether they name it or not
but i do know the name
and it is the
RAINBOW – *Salmonidae*; *Salmo gairdneri*
polyanadromous – steelhead
forget the name – look at the THING
leaper fighter survivor pursuer of the mayfly
and of the nymph
opportunistic and strong and beautiful
toothed yet velvety
alive in the current and electric through the longrod
it hangs in the air
fulfilling the moment

who touches this fish, touches a life

February 3

for purposes of classification differentiation et cetera
the BROWN is
Salmo trutta
but this fish is more than that
and the word
"streamlined"
was coined with this fish in mind

yea, cousin to the rainbowed one
yet with unique abilities and orientation
this one – not the acrobat, but the strongman
and the wiseman
choosing to use strategy and muscle
rather than leaps
to assert his freedom

seldom seen in the spring branch
and still there displaying more caution
staying in the depths
until night removes the anglers
inspiring insecta to danse over the waters

of European heritage
this pilgrim insists upon more skill
and if the fisherpoet is to entreat his presence
a deft presentation
is essential
and must be appropriate
to the
time
place
conditions

and
ineffably in tune with the surroundings
personal and infinite

February 4

altho rainbow is a native american
another shares that distinction
BROOK – *Salvelinus fontinalis*
is the pure cold water seeker of the clan
and does not tolerate change
as do its cousins

smaller more delicate diminishing
colorful sporting and elusive
tester of veracity
notifier of changing conditions
like a canary in a cave

at times greedy
at times finicky as a cat
as noteworthy an ideal
as any could have

to pursue or to peruse
the fisherpoet must abandon
all accoutrements of civilization
head for the frontier
allow for a different
latitude altitude attitude
and forget big fish
this is a special fish
and altho an
old wise weary solitary wilderness-seeking
fish or fisherpoet
      can be found
it is only in one of those places
wherein magic still has resisted
the onslaught of reality
go up in attitude
maintain a good altitude
watch your latitude

and so go north
young man

February 5

and then there is the trout of the american west
CUTTHROAT – *Salmo clarki*
so named because
of all the general color patterns
and specifics of the individuals
this one
displays
red-slashed lower jaws
not, of course, a throat
which would be superfluous
to a dweller in the silence of the wild place
choosy about clarity and cold
shy to invisibility
a reward to an fisherpoet
moving ahead of the throngs of humanity
up up into the mountainous snowmelt
lurking in the undercut banks
belying the capacity of sustenance
waters can give
in a stream barely wider than the cut
and barely deeper
the shy trout waits
for the current to bring nourishment

and it does

February 6

have you met
LAKE – *Salvelinus namaycush*
cousin to the brook being a char
yet opposite in size and waters
togue mackinaw gray

it speaks of mysteries of the depths and darknesses
poundage supersedes subtlety and grace
colors bleached by lack of sun
yet dweller far from maddening crowds
finesse is replaced by muscle
both within the THING
and in any approach to it
northern lights define territorial boundaries
and it lives
among toothed things
and in schools
and only at certain times
at or after ice-out
way up in the alta-lata tudes
will it move toward the
shores
and snowmelt creeks
and seek
communion
with the domain of the fisherpoet

but, at those times . . .

February 7

found only in the coldest highest waters
dwells the grail of trouts
once inhabiting only california
the headwaters of the kern
now distributed but once the
verification that something precious
could be found by those
willing to make the trek
to the rockladenstrewn waters
and pan for the minutest glimmer
of what?
it is GOLDEN – *Salmo aguabonita*
and embellishes its hues and casts

with the glitter of wealth
such a richness
as to be unknown to those
who have not sought the splendor

rare elusive treasured yet just a part
of the wonder
deigning not
to live in highly trafficked turbulence
but in the peace and threat of wilderness

and the only reason to experience the quest
is the quest for experience
for nowhere other than the intrinsic
are the riches to be found
and sometimes it need not be sought
other than to see the dwellingplace
for that is the essence of its being

and there are easier quests
but none more rewarding

February 8

there are others too
LANDLOCKED (but a salmon) – *Salmo salar*
fish of the northeast but a sojourner to
other landlockings
brother to the anadromous ATLANTIC – *Salmo salar*
sojourner of the atlantic from russia to argentina
mysteriously yet predictably

and then the (arctic) GRAYLING – *Thymallus arcticus*
rare and beautiful
freshwater sailfish of dominant dorsal characteristic
one of european cousins:
– *Thymallus thymallus*
"umber" *ombre*

yet violet in cast
so definite in habit and habituation that
in France headwaters
cold and clear are the
zone a l'ombre or "grayling zone"

survivor of Pleistocene ice aged glaciation
it maintains
where purity is maintained

and then
there are hybridized offshoots of the tree
branching to new growths
such as
brownbow cutbow sambow splake tiger trousal
and rarities
such as
GILA – *Salmo gilae*
and SUNAPEE – *Salvelinus aureolus*
and albinistic and melanistic variations
and particular strains
testifying
to the fecundity and variety of creation
with still yet unchangeable essence

February 9

but what of it these names
whether they be descriptive
or connotative
is a truite not still a truite?
whether
truite arc-en-ciel
or
truite brune
or even *truite commun*
?

what of it
and does the living breathing entity
concern itself
with how it is termed
or is that for the convenience
of those who feel they need
to know the difference
to communicate
which
after all
is not the same thing as
to commune

the words of the mentor extrude the meaning
and clarify classification

my glory:
      i am at one with nature

an reply:
      then you are subdividing too much

February 10

oh but what ARE the choices?
be inclusive –
be reclusive –
be decisive –
be revisive –
? . . .
or just BE

well, then, so, if, and, but,
ok.
that means that if i do have choices
then it is up to me
and i need to be up to it
in which case i cannot leave out

other THINGS

and i should start by telling you that
i am no purist nor opportunist
but that i will fish for other than
trout
and i will write other than
pome
and i will use other than
fly rod
and so forth

if you choose otherwise
you have to live with it
as do I

February 11

so i prepare repare repair prepair
other
baitcasting reel fits to rod
holds 100 yards of 14 pound test
and slams plastic worm and lead
into the milfoil
dredges it over rocks and fallen trees
until
with a thump like wile e coyote hitting the end of his line
a LARGEMOUTH bass – *Micropterus salmoides*
strikes and forges into the moil of weed rock and debris
and must be muscled out
so, you see
at times
finesse is not the only answer
and it is wiser to have made preparations
to BE in the world
if the components thereof
are not what was expected
besides

if you are open to the experience
you may just have one

February 12

ah, yes
tis true, tis true
i will take that delicate graphite rod
and spiderwebby leader
and fly tied from exotic fauna of the world
and cast into a stock tank
delicately
so as not to alert or frighten
bluegill – *Lepomis macrochirus*
green sunfish – *Lepomis cyanellus*
channel catfish – *Ictalurus punctatus*
or even carp – *Cyprinus carpio*
now what do you think about that?

oh, there are other ways to surrogate the experience
take SMALLMOUTH bass – *Micropterus dolomieui*
is said to be very
trout-like
in habit
taking flies
habituating clear cold streams
leaping
andmorebut
wouldnt it be sad
to only be considered or appreciated
for the degree of similarity to another
if one has so many good qualities
all one's own
so
when i fish specifically for
whatever
i try to approach the THING on its own terms
and appreciate it for what it is

rather than what i or anybody else
would have it be
;
and so i embrace the diversity apparent
and enjoy
having prepared and anticipated
and carrying no false notions
of any sort of hierarchy
through spheres or ordained on any level

February 13

new roles come to me bidden or not
and i rise to the occasion
with a multiplistic not opportunistic
relish
as the rainbow soars after ingesting a mayfly
i aspire to what i can
and hope for . . .
hope
and look for what is truly there
and see
and feel and think and do

and be

and the simplest thing turns out to be the truest
and it is that which i have prepared for
so i get into the current of life
and prepare to join the cycles
and fulfill the somethingness of life
in whatever way i can
but also the best i can
given whatever i have to work with
extrinsically and intrinsically

and the largest hope i ever want to catch
is just that i be prepared for

oh
surprise joy pain love death growth happiness hunger riches
poignancy stagnancy
variety
spice
life

February 14

a child is born
will he fish
or play the guitar
or be his own person
and learn to BE and DO

if i am to be guide and guardian to this child
as well as father
must i separate within myself the man and the boy that i am
or should i never forget my beginnings and empathize

somehow the classifications of the adjustments
take a back seat to the miracle itself
and wondrous eyes behold a new person
not much larger than the two hands cradling him
as he opens one eye to garner an impression of me
and of his newend world

of a sudden i know
how my father felt
and why he did the things he did
and the zensations of the moment proscribe
      the future and the past in one sweep

and i know

that the child will be fine and that i can be a good father
because the THING
is to

BE and to DO.

i can do that

February 15

i am born anew in the cycle
when my cycle intersects
another in perhaps another stage

it is a reminder and a refresher
and i experience new birth
in my reflections

i see in a new way without
things that i experienced within
and resee
and smile

the meanings are there
if we choose to see them
written in the lines
displayed in the
concentric circular ripples
succeeding the leap or landing
of a trout or a pebble

unity

is what there is
when we can finally see
the essence of diversity
and embrace it

February 16

its time to prepare – the season will be here soon and the tackle must be ready. mail-ordered gear joins old familiar equipment and fills in the gaps created by loss or carelessness. the rods, having been waxed and polished, are inspected once more – even tho guides have been replaced and windings rewrapped and varnished. then they go into their bags and cases truly ready for the coming expedition. flies have been steamed and hackles stand proudly ready to float in a near-perfect drag-free drift over the lie (if, of course, i can manage to execute a near-perfect cast remembering to give that last little flip that throws slack into the leader); reels and lines have been cleaned and oiled to ensure problem-free operation (or at least minimize the chance); leaders have been catalogued and new ones have joined their brethren in the wallet. tippet material has been restrung by running a leather thong through the spools and through rubber washers (through which the leader is pulled to straighten) and tied to a loop on the vest. hemostats, scissors, knives, clippers, pliers, and multi-purpose tools have been attended to and secured in their domains. waders have been checked for leaks (knowing full well that discovery of a leak can only happen in the stream); newly tied flies insist that older more experienced flies move over and make room; experimental patterns (read about in a magazine and of course needing to be tried – at least once) occupy a special box (probably to be forgotten when the hatch is truly on); the landing net is examined for possible breaks (it must be in perfect shape when it is discovered, trout on line, that it has been left in the jeep); the camera gear is repacked (to be left in the jeep intentionally, as it seems to guarantee a lack of anything photogenic); and the mental checklist is itemized for the jeep (noting that tires, oil, significant fluids, and mechanical gee-gaws are in working order, notwithstanding some sort of a surprise concealed for future revelation). finally it is done and all the tackle rests ready. and the red setter watches patiently as this is done for the umpteenth time this month. and as, he knows, will be done umpteen more times before the season. and he watches indulgently, knowing – it will be time when it is time and no amount of preparation can rush or drag the calendar. altho he is polite enough to keep this to himself.

he just lets me know that he knows.

February 17

i am prepared
but the cycle of season has not turned enough pages
i wait
and try to find the purpose of waiting
perhaps it is anticipation
perhaps it is simply to calm
and to avoid a frantic rush
into doing

it rests heavy
        this waiting
and it tries my patience

perhaps i should do something else
and use this time i have
perhaps i should find something worthwhile
and accomplish it

but if i do this i will rob time
from something
for there is enough to fill my days
i just seem rather
to postpone or neglect
that which is not pressing

perhaps i should postpone reverie
and recollection and impatience
and answer duty's call
and attend domestic matters

there is much to be read
there is much to be written
there are missives to all
and a volume to the reader

this uncomfortability should be included also
it is a part of it
it is necessary
not as contrast
but as ballast
else we would sail away in the wind
and not appreciate what is there
when it is

February 18

So many books to read
should i select a classic
or one from
the guilt shelf
(the ones i intended to read
but i dont know if they have anything to offer
to this state of mind i possess)

at times it is better to go back to the old friends
they look worn and impatient too
and though their covers speak of
being exhausted to the point
of not managing duty anymore
they still contain all their old wisdom
and new ideas which were always there
but which i couldn't see until
i had trod many of the same streams as their authors

and so i share memories with Schwiebert
of colorado waters and tricky trout
and i glory in Bergman's solution
to yet one more unique average situation
and i find more in these old worn books
than could ever have been put there
until i could have written them myself
especially the notion

that there are times for angling
and times for reading
and times for poeticizing
and times

February 19

my window shares a branch
now's lack of leaves will abate come spring
and cover the view while richening it
but i will not be here to look through it

i will be on the spring branch
enjoying the blossoming of the season
and casting oiled lines
over winter-hungered fish

my coat hangs on a peg on the back of the door
or is that the front
or the inside or the face or the center
what matters is the coat

it will not be there come spring
nor will i
spring branch awaits restive
and eternal as it must

the books will rejoin their brothers on the shelf
the worktable serves as restingplace for them now
making room for writing and fly-tying and such
to be cleared when its time

and i sit at my chair to do what i can here
and i wear my coat and boots to do what i can there
and i let my chair accept me now
for the time that i will not be here

February 20

Have you considered the possibility
that
you dont have to try all the possibilities
or that
maybe all you need is one possibility
and that
each every and all may be a possibility?

it seems to me

that in the newness of the year
before habit has settled in
is a time perhaps
for making choices
with conviction

and within whatever realm i dwell
i make a new choice
and it suits me
and will

because it is the same choice
albeit different in aspect
as that made by the
tree
trout
triviality
truth

and that is to
GROW

because, oddly enough
tho we have but little choice in the matter
this is essentially
the only choice there to make

i mean – whether or not
because in the end
it boils down that
the choice is really whether
or not
to try

February 21

take a new look at an old thing
      or
           being me,
                (an old thing)
           relatively speaking, of course
look through new eyes at the thing

      and then

look at your
      self

because the realization will
      of course
manifest itself in the notion
      that
you
      or i
           be
a new thing
      (relatively speaking, of course)

but containing at least a snippet
of the essence
of the eternal
      if you look
           through

old eyes at a new thing
>	or
new eyes at an old thing

February 22

and so do i prepare with
>	my books
>	my eyes
>	my tackle
>	my heart
>	my pen
>	my soul
>	my . . . my

all

to embark on the quest
knowing full well
that i can not predict the outcome
but only the effort

but that will be enow

i know that IT is there in the spring branch
waiting as always
for me or you to find
however
and that

it is truly the classic quest and that i may find
>	the holy grayel
>	the seven cite-ies
>	the fountain of you-th
>	the lost continent-ment
>	amelia airheart

or, if i am truly lucky, (relatively speaking, of course)
>	mice-elf

and all the attendant mage-ic that dwells within the

crystalline
altho with the stipulation that i look not for the future within
but for the hear and know

as he said and as i read:

Aye, go a-fysshing with an angle.

February 23

and it is all there before me
the paths have been charted
only my steps may vary
but i walk in the traditional
as did my ancestors
(relatively speaking, of course)

and i wonder if
by accident or design
i sometimes step into the footprints of others
it is not intentional
but then it is probably not accidental
as it is in music
whereby
an accidental is not unforeseen or happenchance
but rather another note
between named notes
and with no name of its own
but just possessing directions
(rather than instructions)
to get to it

C# or Bb
        however
may be an instruction

it doesnt matter always to know the difference
it does matter to know there is a difference

and maybe that will come to me
depending upon key
or scale
or form

and it matters
to never
    be
        too
            old
                to
                    play.

February 24

and i walk the path by the spring branch
tho the season has not yet opened
and i observe the tracksprints
left by other seekers on their way

but they are unbootshaped
and padded or hoofed
and speak to me of
raccoon bobcat deer coyote opossum muskrat duck squirrel
rabbit beaver bear

and i wonder at our various purposes in treading here
semi-simultaneously yet invisible
or is there just a single purpose

and is it
to fulfill a role of the cycle
or of cycles
and if so
be preordained that the path should be followed at times
crossed at others
and sometimes the water entered
or allowing its essence to enter

in order to quench that thirst
or slake that fire

all i want
all i ever wanted
was to BE
odd that it oft-times seems impossible
when it is a possibility

at times it is difficult to forget what has been learned
and keep what has been learned
but that is the necessity
and really
what preparation is all about.

February 25

SCENE 3:
    The old man and the two disciples walk down the path laden with various equipment en route to a stone dwelling by the river. It is the riverkeeper's home and he greets the men warmly and invites them in from the cold to share cider by his fire. The old man places his fishing tackle in a corner and withdraws a leatherbound volume from the bag he carries. The disciples fidget with their tackle and the riverkeeper sits metaphysically on a two-legged stool. Although there is no relation here, the conversation must be reported.

ANGLATOR: Damn Julia Berners!
SPORTSTOR: What?
ANGLATOR: You must mean "who" but that is not as important as "why."
SPORTSTOR: Must you always speak in riddles?
ANGLATOR: Howe maeny fiet hath an fyshe?
SPORTSTOR: I see. Forgive me. I will not ask rhetorical questions unless I want rhetorical answers. I was being

	spontaneous and dull.
ANGLATOR:	And that itself is quite an accomplishment. How do you . . . nevermind! We have other matters to consider. Draw from the spontain of youth while you can and be dull while you can. Some certain sharpening will whet you to an edge suitable for life or fishing. Now consider the angle and the target of that angle and prepare suitable tackle. Take you a fly from the rime.
SPORTSTOR:	Shouldn't I be talking to Cotton about this?
ANGLATOR:	Gather wool for all I care! Now . . . are you ready to listen and learn?
METAPHOR:	Cotton? Wool?
ANGLATOR:	Here, Metaphor. Gather. Be inclusive or at least interpretive.
SPORTSTOR:	I am sorry. I am ready to listen now.
ANGLATOR:	Good. Only by listening can you advance and learn. Now prepare.
SPORTSTOR:	OK.
ANGLATOR:	. . .
	. . .
	. . .
SPORTSTOR:	What?
ANGLATOR:	Did not you listen? Oh, you are hopeless. Now is what you have so use it as best you can. Do what needs to be done. The riverkeeper awaits the coming of the season of the angle and is here to husband the trout until their time. We must sort our tackle and be ready when he tells us that our time is come. Since we must be ready then you must now . . . prepare!
SPORTSTOR:	I see. I am preparing.

METAPHOR: What must I do?
ANGLATOR: Just be yourself.

February 26

do you doubt?
then ponder this –
but never relinquish your doubt:

i am not only reborn in my cycle
but on different planes
within the spheres
and circlings
of other cycles
which i intersect
or parallel

and as mute witness i testify
to what i have seen
through what is seen in me
and i feel
the rebirth
of spirit and flesh
or of vegetable
through the communion
consumption
convocation
coincidence

of all that i see or am
and i can but help to smile
at the enormity of this simple THING
and hold it as best i can
as long as i can
however i can
and leaving it
take it with me

February 27

I feel writerly this morning.
What should that MEAN to you?
You should know something about this –
because changes may be affected
or effected
or included or inclusive
The words may be of another
or an other.
The ideas may be new
or knew.
You may need to look up a definition
or look up to a definite sun
or look up to a de-finite son.
So bear with me (or without me)
or bare with me
your soul
or sole
and . . .

don't worry about it
because
there will be many daze
or days
in which or in witch
or Innwich
I or eye or aye
see or sea or si
that the THING
must be right or write or rite or wright
for you to understand
or to under stand,
and I will try to be . . .
readerly.

February 28

and so i write
as awkwared as it may seem
i try
and hope it reaches
as i hope the cast line reaches the lie

and i have to do this my way
whatever that is
but
im sorry i cant write like you
       but if i did
who would fill that space reserved
       for people who write like you
or the gap to be filled by a person
       who writes like me
            (?)

our standards must be set aside
       indeference to equality
and what counts is
attitude
       not the duckbilled platitudes
towards
DOING
which is, after all
what i wanted to BE

i wanted to be a verb
       not a noun
       or especially a pronoun
            not an adjective
            (such a compulsion to qualify)
all i ever wanted was to
BE
and all i ever wanted to be was
DOING.

February 29

the leap is an arc overshooting the surface
whether it be a leap of logic, a lovers' leap, a frog leap,
    or a leap year
or the leap of a rainbow trout into the air
spraying water
as the sunfire reflects from fish surface and spray
far (relatively speaking, of course) above the earth

and the mere existence of this day
is not as a now and then hindrance to the wait for
    opening day
but part of a natural cycle
or compensation for the authenticity inherent in a
    natural cycle
in which so many days at twenty-three hours
    and fifty-six minutes
add up to one extra day over the course of four years
and keep the day at a reasonable twenty-four hours

but how does the sun know to come up one extra time?
does it do so in abeyance to our rude calculations?

how can this all fit together anyhow
the earth is twenty-four thousand miles in circumference
    or thereabouts
and turns in less than that many hours
as we spin moving a thousand miles per hour
or so it would seem
but we seem to stand still
relatively speaking, of course

we only notice when something moves
or catches our attention
or shows up on the calendar

or odd as it may seem, when we

suspend time as the leap bursts through the surface
scattering spray and color
and stirring within the fisherpoet
a sudden appreciation
for every extra day
no matter
where
it comes from

March

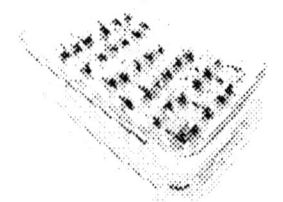

March 1

Opening day

I stand in the water beneath the bridge
Others are there, of course
waiting . . . looking up . . . making ready . . .
to DO

Those in transit cross the bridge GOING
or look over the side in wonder
but those under are in the process
of doing, altho waiting for the time

the rising sun directs its beams and
offers little warmth to those under
standing in the current
feeling icy pressure on legs

then it is open
   I and others cast
      those lucky enough
         find themselves
            gripping with numbed fingers
              a living thing
                  athrobbing with life essence
                  and those who dont
                    realize

they are lucky just to be there

                DOING

March 2

The spring branch has changed little but significantly
        since last seen
The current has poco a poco moved boulders

        and cut channels
New lies have been formed
        old lies smoothed over
hatches are yet to be and nymphs cling to debris

It is not yet time for experimentation
and the fisherpoet applies self to task
employing past successful strategies
        whether self-originated or mined from
        the mother lode of others' past successes

but to new purposes

Old casts go by habit to old lies
and it takes some trial and error to grasp the futility
so a new cast, using an old strategy
goes to a new lie, once then again

And the trick, if it may be called that,
is to reshape old thinking patterns
and to find what will work
in this new yet old environ of the spring branch

nothing more than creative problem solving

March 3

And so

I tie a "new" fly to the leader with shaking fingers
It does not offer more promise than the others—
But it does mean change
Each fisher must start anew with what he has
and with what he can learn
But the choices can be boggling, choosing from the little
soldiers in formation:
(and all must be considered, even though they need not be
called until it is time)

the dries—

Adams	Brown Hackle	Mosquito	White Miller	Grizzly Wulff
Light Cahill	Renegade	Caddis	Royal Coachman	Hendrickson
Pink Lady	Joe's Hopper	Blue Dun	Brown Drake	Black Gnat
Deer Fly	Muddler	Spider	Colorado King	Ginger Quill
Irresistible	Pale Evening Dun	Sofa Pillow	Rio Grande King	Black Ant
Professor	Tup's Indispensable	Buzz Hackle	Wickham's Fancy	March Brown

the nymphs—

Muskrat	Olive	Peacock	Bitch Creek	Brassie
Black Stone	Bristle	Burlap	Brown Bomber	Caddis
Stone	Gray Rat	Hare's Ear	Hellgrammite	Shrimp
Miracle	Spruce	Tellico	Teeny	Zug Bug
Montana	Near Enough	Troth Leech	Green Damsel	Breadcrust
Scud	Green Drake	Yellow Stone	Brown Bastard	Butler Special

the streamers—

Black Ghost	Woolybugger	Platte River Special	Partridge	Sculpin
Silver Spruce	Matuka	Hornberg	Black Bear	Bucktail
Edson Tiger	Bullhead	Marabou	Integration	Muddler
Spuddler	Supervisor	Spruce	Mickey Finn	Gray Hackle
Prawn	Silver Doctor	Coachman	Black Leech	Little Brook
Polar Chub	Shusan Postmaster	Governor Aiken		

and more

March 4

And then there are the variations—
for example:

A Coachman can be royal, leadwing or California
A Marabou can be any color of the rainbow
from fluorescent pink to black, from hot orange to brown
A Wulff can be black or white or royal or gray or blond
      or grizzly or Lee or Joan
or even in sheep's clothing

An Adams can be blue wing, female, spent wing,
      yellow body, hair wing, upright

or any member of the family, including Leticia (or Thing)
And a caddis can be . . . can be . . . so many different things
each to its time and place that books are written just about
        this one

And that doesn't account for size
hooks can vary depending upon the size of the insecta
        at a particular time of the year
or on the particular stream where growth rates vary
or on attractor versus imitation theory

And that doesn't account for variations in materials
one guy uses snippets from his cat
another from his dog
another from his mother's old hat
and yet another from roadkills
more than one raises his own chickens
and some use fibers from the endangered species list
and it goes on and on

Until it finally boils down to the tier and how he binds the
        STUFF together to form . . .

        his own creation

And he could be a Wullf, Hewitt, Walton (Cotton), Berners, Trueblood, Jorgensen,
        or some Joe of the Brooks
Or he could be a Whitman, Crane, Eliot, Doolittle, Williams, Duncan, Kinnell,
        or Dorn, Pound, Ginsberg, Roethke, Merrill, Warren, or Zukofsky.
Or someone else . . .

March 5

I (you) have to choose, sort, separate, integrate, classify, transmogrify, vilify, and yet choose . . .

And I find consternation
    in the differentiation
and what's more—the presentation
    of the
flies, flies, flies, flies, flies, flies, flies.

and so I (you), a clear-thinking problem solver,
    set upon this simple solution:

I will fish dry with only an Adams of various sizes
I will fish nymphs with only a hank of hair
    and a bit of thread
I will fish streamers with an ever-loving Woolybugger—
and by the time I get the various colors and sizes
    toadequately cover the situation—
I find myself with enough flyboxes to choke a horse
(if a horse was ever so inclined)
and my vestment is full
my hackle tackle is plethoric

and I find myself with enough generics to fill the bill under
most conditions and concentrate on the presentation because
the trick, even in the face of all these choices is to
    put the fly in the lie
and to imagine the perspective from the inside
    of the spring branch
and to offer a viable alternative to
what seems to be the natural order of things
but to be in it rather than be an intruder . . .

March 6

but wait—there is further confusion
because in angle-land
where i visited once

there are different names
and for different things, at that
and so
it gets even more muddling
especially considering that
they had no muddler
but
gaping (using proper anglish
and not dropping g's)
made it in canada anyway
and so i jump back
and count again

Red Montana	Booby	Baby Doll	Jersey Herd	Catswhisker
Whiskey	BlackCat Whisker	Floating Fry	Wormfly	Dog Nobbler
Cul de Carnard	Silver Invicta	Sedge Drake	Mayfly	March Brown
Red Ant	Hopper	Damsel	Tupp's	Shipman
BuzzerChomper	All	Still	In	Order

so now what?
i think i will leave them in order
to not add to the confusion
and they can stay
in their soldierly rows forever
i think that would be best
all things considered

March 7

this early in the season
i feel rushed
but try try try to remember
to slow down
and appreciate
anticipate
andenjoy
i cast
trying to avoid a tangle
or a hook in my ear

it is not easy
but i know i can do it
and eventually
remember what i already knew
and knew that i knew
but just forgot
onceagain
that i knew it

and the waters are cold
but not as biting as the air
so it is better to stay in
despite the discomfort

and once i have done
i feel better
having rediscovered my place
and my self's place

and i am rewarded with intangibles
that i can
feel—touch
see—look
smell—inhale
taste—ingest
hear—LISTEN

March 8

as the trout strikes (takes) the lure
he gives
as the fisherpoet lands (takes) the trout
he receives

but between is life
and the connection
tapering to a spidery strand
with the line only as strong

as it is at the finest diameter
when pentametrically opposed
to ponderings by those
who haven't

and maybe never will

i yearn to touch
from one end of the line to the other
and to, as advised,
fish fine and far away
whether here or there
follow that closely

therein lies the key
to investing
and divesting
so . . .

remember
experience

March 9

but wait, you ask—
what of this THING?
is this not some isolationist activity
pursued in solitude
by stoic individuals
who speak in some esoteric jargon
and who move about wild places in silence
at odd hours of the day?

wait, i ask—
don't mistake terms for jargon
they were invented to enhance clear communication
and to help with the remembering
of who or what contributed
not off-putting but clarifying, hopefully

and the times are determined externally
and the places are determined naturally
the only choice is whether or not
to BE there

and the stoicism you speak of
is merely recognizing that one who goes there
does so not under any terms
but those dictated by the time and place

and the isolation you speak of
is quite simply not an accurate depiction
of the attitude shared
by the siblings of the angle
who, each in an own cycle,
savors those moments of intersection
with other cycles
but knows that there is no use
filibustering those who will not hear

and so . . .

March 10

silence is misunderstood.

it is not a rejection but an opening up
to the sounds et cetera that are already there
and it is not intended personally to affront
but as a style of sponging inwardly
all that which surrounds

if i fish for trouts without singing ballads
it does not mean i am not happy—
because i am likely ecstatic
it does mean that i am taking in the whole thing at once
or as much of it as i can
to store for those times when i am

        elsewhere
and if i do not initiate a conversation
it is because i do not want to bore you
with that which is not your way
unless you ask
and then
then
you might not be able to shut me up

March 11

ANGLATOR: Eschew that which will not be of service.
SPORTSTOR: Yes, but if it's not broke, don't fix it.
ANGLATOR: Shhhhh . . .
SPORTSTOR: I don't understand.
ANGLATOR: There are times words will suffice; there are times not. Look into the eye of the hurricane, put a seashell to your ear, lay that selfsame ear to the ground, climb a mountain, love   one who loves you—and simply absorb that THING, that ESSENCE and distill it and carry it with you on the tip of your tongue and in your heart and in the back of your mind and in your outstretched palm . . . and you will understand. Was there ever one of these things that, having done, you said—"I did not need to do this because I read about it and I saw pictures and someone told me about it and it was just like they said it would be."—?
SPORTSTOR: Well, no—I have to see for myself.
ANGLATOR: Aye, there's a double-edged sword. So you DO understand.
SPORTSTOR: I do?
METAPHOR: I get it—seeing is believing.
ANGLATOR: Again you try to put the horse before the cart—Believing is believing without seeing.

	Seeing is seeing. It is so simple it quite amazes me how it eludes you. But, hold—I realized the problem now that I have been caught up in it. Cease this prattle and you will understand.
SPORTSTOR:	But how . . .
METAPHOR:	But what . . .
ANGLATOR:	Shhhhh . . .
SPORTSTOR:	. . .
METAPHOR:	. . .
ANGLATOR:	. . .
SPORTSTOR:	Oh!!!
METAPHOR:	Ah-Ha!!!
ANGLATOR:	Yes!!!

March 12

Something Fishy

I cast a fly upon a brook,
    whereupon a trout took
I played the fishy very well
    and heard the pealing of a bell.
Why do these things seem so the same?
    I didn't know before I came.
And what am I to do with this:
    a thought that this that matters is
Important in so many ways,
    now and in my later days.
If I be granted just one wish.
    it would be for more days to fish—
And maybe once to look with eyes
    that see and be and realize.
That would be quite enough to ask—
    a noble quest; a lifelong task.

(whew . . . im glad thats over)

March 13

Superstitious?
        then stay home.
                                or
do you just believe in things that you can't see?
there is a difference, you know . . .

                i believe in
                    love
                    angels
                    gravity
                    time
                    happiness
                    sadness
                    hunger
                    gods
                    goddesses
                    ambition
                    peace
                    future
                    past
                    air
                    infinity
                    relativity
                    santa
                    jesus
                    atoms
                    hope
                    now
                    &
                    you.

March 14

let's go fishing
i know a place
and it will be all the better
for having shared it with you
it takes some traveling to get there
and a faith that it will be good
but it is better anyway to have tried
than to have just stayed
so
come with me
to the spring branch
and tie an adams to your leader
and pull enough line from your reel
to cast to a prime lie
let it drift without drag
over a feeding trout
and
hopefully
the trout will accept your offering
in the spirit in which it was intended
and not with a sense of duplicity
and hopefully
you will accept my offering
in the spirit in which it was intended

March 15

have i made you laugh yet?
good
for at times it is good to laugh
and at times it is good to cry
and you will
but please dont ever forget especially—
one law of physics
that
for every force

there is an equal
and opposite force
and i think that is ok
i have laughed and i have not
it balances
i roll with the bad times
anticipating the good
enjoying what is there
for the time that it is not
orbits, though elliptical
maintain a balance
and a cycle does not need to be
a perfect circle
that would not be human
and i am
but a cycle also cannot have square corners
spring turns into summer
see?
and there will be another spring after this one
and there was one before this one
and it will continue
with or without
you or me
augurers did not need to be
quite so mysterious as they pretended to be
it takes no great power to see—
only a willingness
so
i guess you could
beware the ides
but isnt it also possible
to look forward to them?
at any rate—to anticipate?

March 16

there is nothing more satisfying than watching steam rise
from my socks as i lean my chilled feet upon the andirons.

warmth soaks through the wetness and feet that had been numbed by wading in the icy spring branch begin to tingle as feeling comes back. the day was very cold and ice formed in the guides and along the line when it hung in the air. fingers in fingerless gloves could sometimes not tell the difference between shivering and a trout taking a deeply drifted nymph. now, in front of the friendly crackle of the fire, with hot chocolate and warming feet, i can reflect on the day. there were seven trout in the morning, the first hooking himself on the fly and beginning a run before i even knew he was there. i actually even heard the ratchety whine of the reel before i felt the fish through the graphite rod. i moved and reflexed in slow motion but the trout's faculties were intact. luckily i had started the day with a heavier tippet than normal, just because i was afraid of losing a fly and having a hard time tying on another with shivering hands. the irony of fishing this time of year is that waters that could chill to numbness during july now thaw fingers and make them function again, provided they are dried quickly. i played the first trout awkwardly, letting him run up down and across the current. i did not care if the other trout in the pool were spooked—i would let this fish run and enjoy his wild free rushes and leaps. when he became tired, i eased him alongside and pulled a glove off with clattering teeth. the slowly moving hand did not frighten him and as i brought it up under the trout, he just relaxed and lay cradled in my palm. i tucked the rod under my arm and eased the fly from his jaw with fingertips not gloved and then lowered the fish back into the water. i paused for just a moment to admire the colorings of this fish, so completely different than any other of his species, yet marking him as a rainbow. it took a few seconds for him to realize that he was again free and he slowly swam out of my hand and turned in the current. there was no loss of dignity in his defeat; next time he could be the winner in our contest, and the leisurely quality of his swimming after release seemed to indicate that he knew this. six more trout came to my fly that day—none stronger or more beautiful than the first, but each with certain qualities of its own. all were released back into the spring branch to return to the point of the cycle where they had been interrupted. after a time, so did i return with a leisurely walk to the cabin where i stoked the fire, warmed my feet, drank hot chocolate and reflected on the day while the red setter breathed steam on the windowpanes.

March 17

its good to be irish, or at least partly irish on this day
the wearing of the green presupposes the coming of the green
and gives hope and cheer
good spirits abound and we partake
the colleen shares a coffee with me and we let the trout rest for now
this is a time for dancing, and i learn to move my feet
in harmony with the earth and in time to the music
1-2-3-4-
how deep the color in her eyes
how beautiful her long hair
5-6-7-8-
how like a feather she floats sensitive to the rhythms
how twinkly her eyes when the smile spreads across her face
9-10-11-12-
how she moves with her own spirit yet with mine
how she eases closer with each turn
13-14-15-16-
how she moves with tiny graceful feet
how she glides next to me

and we part after the dance
and if we never meet again
at least we had this day
and this time and place
to be irish for a day
and could look forward
to the coming of the green

March 18

"Well"
sez yr humble fisherpoet
"Where do we go from here?"

we have been to the branch
and in the water's current
and have caught the first trout
(could there ever be 'nother like that one)

do we look for new things
or new ways for looking
or look at things we knew
or take the things we looked at?

are we progressing
or did we hit a meteor with our cycle
that jarred our orbiting sphere into a different plane
are we truly seeking progression
or trying to recreate that first feeling

when we newly looked experienced felt knew
that which would define latter days?

how can you know
when you are in it
if you are on the line
however curved, that it is straight
if it can only be seen looking back?

the only qualification i can now make
is that i follow my heart
and the rest of me tags along
and even if i cant see
at the time
ultimately i will
one makes mistakes

n-n-no-one makes n-n-no mistakes
i do the best i can.

March 19

i wonder if there was ever
so dedicated an angler as me
i stay up all night
to not miss the sunrise
for that is the time to catch trout
and i will freeze myself standing in the cold air
along the spring branch
calculating the perfect approach
with the most potential
and remembrancing all i have read
from technical tomes
about
flies lies water current temperature insecta
        cycles

i brave the elements to match my wits with
well . . .
a creature with a brain
roughly the size of a pea
and revel in my abilities
when i catch one
after another
after another

simple creature
though beautiful
and in sufficient numbers
duly logged into my journal
reveal further information
of those times
when i can most likely catch more

i change

flies leaders lead line depth approach position
technique and location
to catch more
because . . .

i like to
or i need to
or i want to
or i have to
and there you have it.

March 20

Forget this artsy-schmartzy-crafty stuff—
I fish with a fly-pole because
it is the most efficient manner
with which to take trout

And I take them in numbers
If they matter, then read my journal
It doesn't lie because only truth and standards matter
And a skilled angler
Which of I am wherefore one
Needs naught but the truth
No exaggerations here—
Just the facts.

I can quantify my successes
and quantize my results
and formulate tactics for
reading the stream
using all the data at my command
and catch more fish than many
And with confidence enow to bet
on the results of a day on the stream

What do you say?

March 21

what am i saying?
WHAT am i SAYING?

this is not why i want to fish
why did i do that?
what circles did i run in that
made me think numbers matter

i realized this one day
when i had to stop
because it was no longer fun
it was predictable
it was
boring
it
was
meaningless

and so i hooked the *Tricorythodes* to the keeper
and went back to the bank
to get a perspective
and walked
and stopped on the old stone bridge
in the center
and looked
and saw
things that i had been too preoccupied to notice before
because they disturbed my focus
now i look
and see
and one of the THINGS that i saw
was that i needed to acquire some skills
before i could understand the responsibility
in those skills
and those kills were sacrifices through me
as part of a cycle i could not see yet

until i looked backward
and
forward
a little.

March 22

now i can view the new season
with anticipation
and relish each moment
having remembered
there is a purpose to everything
including DOing, BEing,
making misTAKEs,
and LEARNing
sometimes it is difficult
to AVOID a wrong path
by taking the adVICE
of others
the right path is right there
it too must be absorbed through experience

i go to the cabin
with my humbleness in hand
and i wonder who determined
this sequence of learning
it could be A DAMn site easier
eveN if we (thats you & I, mainly)
could learn a few things
from sage counsel.

March 23

Balance restored
    at least from this perspective i
        go to the spring branch
            with an open heart
                and mind refreshed
                    or ready to be refreshed
I take my time and cast gently not hurriedly or anxiously
    (I cringe when I hear someone BE "anxious" to DO)
the air is warmer but the water stays the same
                          i realize and accept
                    that my totem animal
              is still a soaring hawk
        not diving speedily
    just soaring peacefully
on a thermal updraft

March 24

i watch the beginnings
        (op. def.: that point in another's cycle
            where I arbitrarily started)
of the insecta inhabiting the stream at this time
just a few
but there

and i see other fauna
stirring in the shadows of rocks
and logs
and early flora

        and   take   my   time

there is no hurry
for a cycle
will go round
from where it starts

to where it finishes

the catch is that
it is not easy
to draw inferences
of the circumference

without a perspective

March 25

the pool is deep
deeper than the riffle
and the lie may drift
in different depths
fish accordingly
and try
different depths
using what you have

change lures
add lead
lengthen/shorten line
cast elsewhere

perhaps it is
just under the surface
but possibly
it is deep and hidden

it is there
somewhere
to be found
or sought

vary the presentation
find one that works
stay with it

trust it

until it is completed
then move
or change
or rest

but
remember the pool
is different from
the riffle

March 26

i saw the trout suspended
in the . . . clear water
(not gin, not crystal, not air, it is . . . clear)
and i watched it long enough to recognize
this trout among trouts
not large
just individual
and i watched the timing
of the feeding cycle
and watched the drift of
possible foodthings
to and past this trout
i calculated the drift
of my fly
to and past this trout
for several casts
(if i could be that lucky)
and finally
to and not past
as it inhaled my offering
"zing" went the leader tight
and "ratch" went my reel
as the trout erupted
in leaps and runs

and "open" went my mouth
in wonderment
at the marvel of this moment
and of tagging
my own
piece of the mystery
specifically

March 27

sometimes i wander from the bridge
altho it is a wondrous pool
but there are other such places
and riffles too
that contain their own
questions and quests

the easy way is downstream
the current makes walking less pressured
muscles do not strain
but i notice that i face the trout
head-on
and they seem peevish
that i should approach them
so obliquely
so bluntly
they scatter
and move from the lie to the hidey-hole
and put a stop to my notions
of ease

i turn

and head upstream from the bridge
the going is tougher
i face the current
it pushes constantly
relentlessly

as the water builds momentum
from a low falls
but under that very falls
in the richly oxygenated water
is a hidden lie
i find it
and its possessor
and work it
with varied technique
until the strike
and the play
and the bringing to the surface
and the moment of appreciation
and the release

March 28

you know,
there's a funny thing about good lies
it seems that even tho the user may move on
another will take its place
for a good lie
is still a good lie
and can be used over and over
how strange that one never notices
that the last one to use that lie
got caught
as did the one before that
and the one before that

but a good lie perpetuates
only changing if the current changes
or if dredging has totally altered the environ
in which case

a good lie will still be found nearby
because it profits
and it may be just slightly removed

but in actuality
still there in toto

so
i (through experience)
try to remember the characteristics
of a good lie
and keep my eyes open
and recognize when i see one

and present my own artificial offering
with subtlety
and humility
aware of my part in this bargain

March 29

a novice
a neophyte
a tyro
a dub i am

there is so much to learn
and never
enough time

and yet

i have to have to have to
make mistakes to truly learn
and even if that is not a waste of time
it still seems . . .
i n e f f i c i e n t
to have to go through that

especially
knowing that i may have to go several times through
but

what can you do?
try
and agin try
and agin
and hope that it can be sorted

it is possible
(sad but true)
to become locked in a cycle of error
just as in a cycle of progression
and to commit the self-same judgementally wrong THING
endlessly
and to be
an experienced
        novice
        neophyte
        tyro
        dub

break the cycle of necessary error
by LOOKING
        and REMEMBERING

March 30

the season opens
        full of hopes
        insecurities
        anticipation
        budding awareness

and knowing that the only way to gain enough experience
(in order to correct wrong thinking)
is to keep DOING and BEING
and the fisherpoet
takes graphite in hand
and applies substance
in whatever proportions seem to work

but not, possibly never, knowing for sure
but adding the clues
and recognizing feedback
when the lure is taken
the hook set
the line tightened and
the quarry landed

early in the season
the cycles are not apparent
yet.
the poetfisher takes time
when it can be had
and comes as close as any scientist
to holding a piece of it
strangely
it is not heavy
it is light
but not fragile at all
when taken on its own merits
it is only when loaded down
with unnecessaries
that it becomes heavy

at this time in the season
and early in the day
misconceptions can be lain aside
in favor of now
without then intervening

March 31

so the first part of the season has passed
things are now in full swing
the path is now open
and the buds now burst

herein is found the crossroads

not necessarily four paths
but maybe
it could be three
which is the three-way junction
known as *tri-via*
now what does that imply?
part of the *trivium*
including
the three-fold way
of
        grammar
        logic
        rhetoric
now what does that imply?
what is trivial to one
        may not be
to
        another.
eh?

April

April 1

The cruelest month, so I'm told
                        by a poet who never wet a line –
    Did he have an income tax deadline to meet?
It seems as though spring has come
                and snowmelt loads the freshets with runoff
And fills the fields with the beginnings of columbine
                and the spring branch with sustenance for
Trout who seem to somehow know that
            it is time to be arise.

Izaak could have told him
           if he would have but listened,
that there are more important things astir
           in heaven and on earth
than are dreamt of by bank fishermen.
                get into the current – feel the cold power
fish deep, drifting a nymph or streamer
            through the pools, just in case –

It may be true that God does not subtract
                from the number of our allotted days,
Those days spent fishing.
                Noah must have caught quite a few,
because he lived for centuries –
                I wonder if he trolled a streamer
from the stern of the ark
            but, if so, how many cubits deep?

April 2

do you wonder that
He and the disciples were fishers?
have you perhaps missed something in that message
could it be a path to grace or salvation
rather than or in addition to
what non-fishers think

when they decry the fact that a sunday morning
may be spent in pursuit of a hobby
instead of something more MEANINGFUL
cast your critical eye toward this:

but of course, the purpose of fishing is fishing, not catching
its what we have instead of Yahweh
isnt it charming to cognate it thusly
well, on the seventh day one should rest, you know
hasnt that behaviour been modeled for us
observe god's dress code
wear your chest waders into the chapel
and into breakfast
baptize yourself in the water
shall we gather at the spring branch
or should we just stay home
or should we go crazy
all i need is a guitar and a fishing rod and this ash tray and a coffee cup and . . .
oh – say a million bucks – and i will feel like a king
hows that? with your fingers?
ha!
jerk
dont try it if you havent knocked it

April 3

the notion of rebirth on a sunday morning
is no news to the fisher
or the poet
who both have celebrated the glory of creation
where it is found

and who both revel in miracles
and who are closely attuned to life cycles
and who have come to terms with death
and rebirth

what then do you make of a fisherpoet
who seemingly combines all aspects
of the pursuit of the trivial

is affirmation of life relegated
to only conventional occupance

or is this truth founded upon faith

but the fisherpoet does not need to be understood
he only needs to DO and to BE

and the fact that he pauses to reflect
or to express
only indicate a sharing nature

and criticism is neither invited nor accepted
because it simply implies
that the critic cannot understand
having postulated from a narrowed posture

celebrate rebirth and be accepting
of all who seek – however oblique their course may seem
there is a time for everything and another turn of the wheel
may put you on the outs as you once were
or did you forget

April 4

better cast
experience
smoother line
dragless drift

confident rise
against the current
smooth take
timed cycle

leap
appreciation
kinesis
elemental touching

feathered lure
intersecting cycles
sensual realization
hope

April 5

dogwoods bloom in the ozarks
telling me things – secrets and memories;
if i pursue trout
i miss the incomparable crappie spawn

those whitebloomed trees remind me of days when
as a child
i watched for the bobber to sink and set the hook delicately
and pulled a warmwater slab to the surface

simple joy of spring but
those days are gone – those shared times
have passed
i fish for other reasons now

but still i hear the trees
luring me with constancy and nostalgia
and i turn the opposite way at the intersection
and head for the spring fork

where the stream enters into a warm lake
trout disdain water of this nature
but crappie line up like commuters
in a cycle of spawning

i put the styrofoam float on the line
about a foot or so above the marabou
and roll cast to the edge of a sunken locust tree
the float goes under immediately

sophistication is not always required
for simple joy
i have fun and the boy inside says
thanks for bringing me back here today

April 6

ANGLATOR: Do you realize that . . .
these tales of rebirth are rather transparent? Like the shallows, they contain simple truths that hold without reminder. Your point is well taken and quite true, but a more subtle approach might serve better.

METAPHOR: Sorry. I get carried away. Conceit sometimes gets in the way. I will speak more universally in particular but try to be approximately more exact. Will that help?

ANGLATOR: Who knows? Just be more purposeful and guiding.

SPORTSTOR: Have I done anything to offend? I merely try to apply what I have learned and hope to progress.

ANGLATOR: You are fairly well equipped so make use of your supply. Find a way to make use and sort the paths. Despite appearances, not all are the same. Not all are wrong; not all are right. All, however, offer learning. Now is the time. There are always steps to take and things to do. You will realize if you veer to a temporary path.

April 7

so i went west
following those dreams
that lead to whatever
and i learned along the way
but i didn't find
anything
i didn't know that at the time
because i thought it had to be there
somewhere
perhaps in the platte river
or the blue
or lurking in one of those famous rivers
flowing from a famous mountain source
of which writers write
and photographers photograph
i dressed the part
just in case
those rivers were generous to me
they gave me trout and memories
they offered awakening of a sort
they gave me scars
but they didn't kill me.

April 8

the green flows through
wyoming utah colorado
it is cold and swift and like some i have known
changes character at times
but it is still the green
to me it was a source of
large trout
to be taken on the fly
i watched the river and saw it rise
and saw three casting on the other side
become trapped

and try to get back
but too late
the current rose in proportion
to the rise in water
which rose in proportion
to the turning of a turbine
which responded to a computer
in altogether a different state
and was unreachable by phone
these three tried to cross the torrent
and lost their cooler in the effort
and one became lodged on a
semi-sunken boulder
in the river
finally
we got a raft and lights and ropes and
by putting in upstream could cross
and bring them back
and i wondered later
if they had even been on the same river
that i had fished as i saw them cross.

April 9

i fish for life
and wonder about death
a nest sits in the cleft of a cliff
across the river from where i cast
of all things, baby buzzards stand in a line
watching me
i had never seen their like before
or even thought about them
even once
but these birds could not spring full-grown
from nothing
at one time these omen-birds were innocent babes
cute to their mother — (i would assume)
and playful and curious as well

but they are marked and destined from inception
all life seems then to be so marked
what it will eventually be
it already is
i don't ask the birds if they want to change
or if they have any concept of a different life
i just watch them
and they me
i think about how lucky i am to be fishing
on such a day
secure in my cycle
enjoying the choices that i have made
employing my free will.

April 10

i stalk the stream
a blue heron
perched
looking
for that shadow that signifies

a particular trout
of such size
as to be a worthy
quarry

blend in with surroundings
camouflaged motionless slowly
the shadow may only be a part
differentiated from the rippled reflection

turn of head ingesting
flick of tail maintaining
sideways shift
momentary elevation

infinitely
slow
movement
into position

cycle timed – cast made
again again again again
perfectly more than once
but not always

cycles intersect – lure takes hold
heaviness beyond anticipation
adrenalins flow
struggle, not epic, but classic

hearts pounding
landed
intimate awareness
release

April 11

the quest for a trout
of monster size (relatively speaking, of course)
insists on disdaining trout of smaller size
specialization creates aloofness

the challenge of such a trout
leads to madness of a type
welcome yet draining
and sets apart those who seek

silence characterizes the hunter
stalking must be done in solitude
joviality is reserved for appropriate times
care is afforded every last detail
the fisherpoet searches for that right word
one that has ne'er been used in the context

one that will send readers on a subsequent search
for meaning

and beneath the bridge as well as acrost it
are remembered the footsteps of those who sought
in their time and in an individual way
before hooking a particular truth

is such a quest purposeful in itself
or is it confirmation that the need to know
can find the one among many
who may carry the secret?

April 12

i seek new waters
but so did Ponce de Leon
he may have been under a mistaken notion
regarding how to extract the elixir
from the fountain
drinking the water was not a good idea then
nor is it now, tho for different reasons
i do understand something about him
i'll bet he knew all the time that what he sought
like the philosopher's stone or the holy grail
could not conceivably be found
but i'll bet he had more fun looking
than he would have had without searching
for the revitalizing waters –
he probably understood
that what he sought was there
in every spring and fountain and pool
but especially in the search –
my own baptism occurs again and again
my renewal, physiological and symbolic,
comes to me from the waters
i am cautious about where i drink
but i absorb as much as possible

i thank all the waters
for in the scheme of things
at one time past or at some time in the future
the water i see may constitute an ocean
or a river or rain or a tear
i'm sure Ponce smiled to himself
the entire time
and never let on
he just kept looking

April 13

what
exactly
if anything
in your opinion
constitutes
a
worthy purpose
eh?

if it be fame
then St. Peter welcomed Atilla
as he did Gandhi
or might it be wealth
then Buddha greeted Midas
and recycled – well, me among others
once there was a notion
that intent could be read upon the quality of the features
you know – ugly is as ugly does
i suppose there were no tabloids at the check-out stand
during the renaissance

what if . . .
this is all there is
or ever will be
who would hear my prayers then?
i would

because i would live as i live
seeking what is there
in any case
finding my own personal heaven
with its own entrance requirements

belief
awareness
constancy
devotion

April 14

have you ever seen a boundary on the ground?
i think boundaries are imaginary limits placed on constructs
by people who have most likely never been there

people die over boundary disputes
and when it is over what
if anything
has actually changed
except the location of an imaginary construct

do you have boundaries?
are they imaginary?
do you put limits on constructs
whether you have been there or not?

do you call your boundary:
reality.
if so, then what do you do with your beliefs?
do they fit into
reality
or are they just something you place beside it?
my reality is comprised of
land and water and life
my boundaries are my limitations
my beliefs are what i do

what i do is who i am
who i am is what i will be
what i will be is where i start
it
is
a
cycle
and as sure as there is a god in heaven
i am who i am
and i try

April 15

taxed to the utmost,
i put one foot in front
      of the other
and trudge back from
      where i have had to go
at least it is easier to get back
      than it was to get to

the sense of accomplishment is,
      of course,
counterbalanced by
      the cost

i wonder if a sense of balance occurs
      across the board
i dont mind paying my fair share
      not at all

the wondering of balance occurs
      about those warders
and whether or not they perceive that
      they must use only their fair share

too many times i have seen fishers
      using and keeping

as though a resource were infinite
>and meant only for their usage

take should balance with need
>even if not all need yet
there will be a future
>and there will be future need

April 16

having paid my allotted share i go a-fishing. the spring branch is inviting and buds on the redwoods and dogwoods hint that life is easing toward fruition. i check the tackle carefully as i always do early in the season. the rod is flexed the leader and line are straightened oiled and where the fly joins the leader the knot is tested and found to be solid. i wade into the stream and enjoy that sudden moment when i realize that my waders are not going to leak at least not this time and i look as i ease into the place in the current where i see that i can cast to the prime lies. for a moment i suspend and just look. a smaller trout works near the overhanging rocks possibly finding the odd surface-trapped bug but more likely plucking nymphs from just under the surface. as they are dislodged from their rocks they tumble in the current and sometimes as apparently now roll close to the surface where trout slurp them exuberantly. then i see a flash deeper in the current and notice another larger trout turn its side as it takes a deeper nymph. it is confirmed then and i applaud my foresight at tying on a nondescript nymph before coming to the stream. i do add some lead to the leader and prepare to lure deeper larger fish. and then i watch some more. hearing a splash i look upstream expecting to see the ripples of a recently leaping trout but it is the red setter. he learned his stream etiquette early and plays in a riffle far from where i am fishing. we can fish an entire stream this way respecting each other's purpose and leaving undisturbed pools for each other. he has better manners than some people i have run into. seeing a flash in the current i look closely and make out the shape of a large trout a very large trout barely visible against the mossy rocks. i observe the current and anticipate the drift and watch the trout for his feeding rhythm. when i think i have calculated well i cast. nothing. and nothing as i cast again and on for an hour. i vary the lead the drift the cast the presentation. nothing. but somehow i have not alerted this fish. perhaps it is confident in the prime lie and views my efforts with disdain from the depths. then one of the turns in the current seems to be concurrent with my nymph. i repeat the cast and another turn. and again. and again. and then the fly is taken and i feel the fly rod throb with the power of a large a very large trout. now strategy takes over. keep the fish headed upstream put pressure on when it goes for a downed log stay downstream from the fish ease the pressure when it runs. the leader is solid the reel drag is lubricated the oiled line slides through the rod guides. i feel the runs grow shorter and the plunging and leaping diminish. finally it comes to my net and i glory in that indescribable feeling of having accomplished. the red setter shares my joy wordlessly but with enthusiasm. this very large trout measurable in pounds rather than inches marks my passage to hunterfisher of exceptional trout. my estimation of self-image is further confirmed later when i bring to net a still larger trout making this a once in a lifetime day. even before i land that trout however i already feel that i have graduated that the spring branch has been outgrown and that i will need to seek other waters. nothing however will reduce the joy the setter and i share on the banks of the spring branch.

April 17

my mentor stands upon the bridge
going neither way but centered
and overlooking the waters
he speaks when i have done

and tells me of moving
he offers me a celebratory drink
but cautions me
not to overindulge

be discerning

but connect

and i tell him that they told me
    drink the beaujolais down
he chides me
    what? too many lay down
    drink of the spring branch, of the blue hole,
    and taste of the purity the earth offers

he informs me
    observe the rainbow
there are no trout in the red river
    but in the blue the green the white
        and the yellowstone
if you seek the rainbow go beyond the horizon
and immerse yourself with it

but read your bowditch carefully
learn navigation by the refraction of stars
know the currents and the depths
step softly
yet
firmly

April 18

i am centered
what a day for fishing
spring runoff swells the branch
caddis and mayfly larvae cling swim tumble
trout feed
i watch
and wait
i look
closely
at the
movement
within the
cycles
i choose
a best fly
i cast
to the
cycling
fish
but do not
catch one
so i move
to a new
location
always
hopeful
observing
absorbing
living
until i
feel that
i have
become
part of the
cycle
my own
centeredness
aligns
and i
fish
catching
or no

April 19

sometimes life is too fragile to survive
and just eases out
unstoppable

a tiny trout hooked just so
is sometimes not able to survive
and there is nothing to do

of course i do not have a plan
or system to deal with this
it is just one of those things

and i do not know if my responsibility
indicates any sort of blame
just perhaps accomplicity

but i mourn his spirit
as deeply as anyone can
and i feel the loss doubly

not only for him
but for us left behind
and for the fact

that he will not swim and grow
and learn and thrive
in the spring branch

April 20

follow the arc created by noah as he casts with his flyrod
his precision follows the timing of a clock
his profile reveals positions on the face of that clock
he stops at two and then pushes forward
tick

tick
paul avoids the world and the pleasures of the flesh
        the devil you say . . .
he casts out what he can but
what're ya gonna do?
fishing can be challenging
but catching can be even more difficult
especially when working without a net
jesus, what a fisherman
tick
tick
timing is everything
if i had been born in another era
perhaps i never would have gone to the spring branch
i might have been distracted
but i think i would have fished
i think i might have written proems
i think i would have loved and felt
tick
tick
cycles are eternal
theoretical circles are perfect
i am not
but i am
i BE
i DO
i would have been a fisherman
i am a fisherman
i will always be
a
fisherman

tick

tick

April 21

i am not sure whether
    i would consider it an honor or not
if, upon reaching my prime –
i were taken from my environment
    as a trophy.
once it seemed a noble enterprise
    to put one on the wall
    but no more

if my only purpose on the planet
    is was replication of my DNA
then i have done that
    the message has been sent
    a cycle has been continued
but if there is something else i can do
    for my own sake or for the sake of others
then i would like to go on a little further
    at least until i feel done

if
    if
i were a large trout
    having reached completion of the circle,
    being destined for another's food chain
even then,
    would i rather continue to swim
    and feed in the spring branch
but
    those days are gone
    when the hunter hunted mainly for subsistence
the reasons for gliding a canoe
    up to a complacent bull moose
    and assassinating him in the shallows
    now are only to decapitate and mount him

          on the wall
a trout does more good in the stream
          under a drowned tree
          swimming and feeding
          than it ever could on a pine board
a trout does more good in my memories
          as i recollect how full of life and beauty
          strength and purpose
i can hope for no less for the trout or myself
          there will be no more trophies on my wall.

April 22

i didn't learn about trophie hunters philosophically
i did that
i pursued larger fish without any concept of food
i wanted proof and validation
i wanted one for the wall and then
i wanted another and another

it took some time to understand nourishment of the soul
it happened after i had filled a wall with lunkers
it made me regret the killing for a while
it did finally turn to peace when
it became apparent that
it was a process that had to be lived to be understood

be aware along the way
be forgiving of your own mistakes
be fair in assessment
be liberal in attitude
be honest in appraisal
be better in time

do what you must in your growth
do what you can to improve
do something – even if it is not perfect
do what all have to do to learn

do until you cannot anymore
do unto others . . .

April 23

the fisherpoet was not born with vision
but did not reject it when it was recognized
      the same is true for the best people i know
      the reason they know so much now
      is that they made many mistakes then
      and learned from them
fair enough –

as a simple soul, i try to eschew the elaborate
      philosophically and practically
i empathize with the trout
      especially the larger ones
      as i grow older
they have their answers, i think –
      or possibly they have no unnecessary questions
they make mistakes in judgement
      when greed overtakes experience
      and i have been known to capitalize on that
others have done as much for me
      and i learned from the pull of the hook

sometimes belief is not a strain
      it just comes with having done
      and having seen
it is acceptance of the way things are
      without argument
to swim in the branch feeling the cool of the spring
      is enough
it is acceptance without judgement
it is fulfillment.

April 24

hey, bud –
wax philostoical on yer own time
this dont have to be so heavy
quicher talkin it and start walkin it
if you want me to buy into this

let go and have some fun
just doit
go fishin if youve a mind to
fergit about the chores
theyll be there tomorrow
knock off all that stuff
and do a pome
that i might like
about purty water and fishies
and purty women and guitar pickers

blow out them cobwebs
and do whatcher tryin to tell about
show me – im from missoura

i quit countin the beat
when i could feel my feet move
now let me show you bout stuff
see that there stream?
git init
feels good – dont it?
look at them trouts
theyre afeedin
cast that flypole over yonder
doit agin and agin
hey
you got one!
what do you think about that?
– no, wait –
dont tell me

just do whatcher doin
n ill watch
til i watched enough
n then ill go git my own fish
savvy?

April 25

i went from the blue to the green to the yellowstone
from the flaming gorge to the firehole
from bonner pass to bennet spring
from aye to zed
from nuts to soup

—

to the thing
and the differences were good
even if i couldnt tell the difference
and the variety was good
even when the same

—

it is finding that one piece of the puzzle
that fits anywhere
that makes the search purposeful
and makes it logical
to answer one question with another

—

trophies have their place
it's just not on the wall
it's in the soul
and in the change in approach
that comes with experience

—

my mistakes are trophies
i learned from them more than from my successes
but i dont really want them around to look at
i internalize and carry them

just so i avoid a cycle of error, if i can

    —

my best trophy is my belief
because it is mine alone
i dont hang it on the wall
i wear it like a fine watch, not flashing it,
but having it ready under my sleeve

    —

just in case you ask me
what time it is

    —

April 26

spring makes things green
before they blossom
people too
i was green as grass once
and now i'm a bloomin whatever
i surely dont have all the answers
about all i can say
is that i know more than i knew then
that is enough

the tree outside my cabin window
has slipped into budding
without ceremony
if pomp is necessary
under the circumstances
then i celebrate my gradualization
in a diplomic manner
hoping i have replaced my ignorance
with wasdumb

i shove aside
philostrophic considerations
and wander out the door
hat on head, coat over arm, red setter at my side

and commune with my tree
it is nameless, but i know it well enough
in its gentle way it has shown me
and i wish to return the consideration

April 27

i wondered about
PEWSAGL
you know, the seven deadlies

pride – i have had, but try to avoid
envy – not much, but some
wrath – only when surprised
sloth – in some ways, but not what i consider the important ones
avarice – overtook me when i didn't know the difference
gluttony – once in a while
lust – i have been in, once or twice

so i wondered about
EARTH-AIR-FIRE-WATER
and asked myself
is this all there is?

without getting boggled down by numbers
i noticed
that there are seven bad things to do
but only four things to do them with
what in the world (relatively speaking, of course)
can that imply?

perhaps it just means that there are more things to be done
than one with each thing
perhaps it is a matter of interpretation
or individuation
so you choose your deadly and
i'll choose mine

take more if you feel versatile
but think about the ratio
of doing:things

offer your opinion, if you must
as to how many gods there may be
and how many beliefs
then explain that ratio to me
explain how any one
can be any better
than any other.

April 28

or chuck it all
and go fishing
on a sunday morning
if you are so inclined
there is baptism and holy waters
if we belief they are
and many do
i think so

how about you?

i climbed a mountain
and found the source
i stood there in awe
seeing the basin

lightning-struck trees
surrounded me
had anyone seen
what had happened here?

how about you?

i cast upon the snowmelt waters

clear as air
suspended trout rose

it could be in solitude
or shared
but i found my ideals
in such a world

how about you?

altitude beckons
vision reveals
quests hearken
souls fly free
how about you?

April 29

first editions sit reverenced on a shelf
held carefully lest they devalue
i keep fishing editions in my backpack
and pencil notes in the margins

my friends are not the perfect ones
they are stained and torn and worn
and spilled upon
but look how much they have done for me

my immaculate collections must be protected
rather than used
how better to be used again and again
than to be useless

i am not a first edition; i am a reprint
of an abridged version
issued by a publisher of limited resource
but no less dedication

what makes me different, i hope
is that in spite of the wear
and the appearance
and stains from spillage . . .
what makes me different, i hope
is the profusion of pencilled margin notes
explaining, mentioning, comparing,
noting, developing, pointing out –

being/doing

April 30

i sum up
it is time to go west again
other waters await
it is time to seek a new perspective

i pack the jeep
the setter sits with cocked head
wondering about this notion
but ready to go

i recite to him:
      "Whan that Aprille . . ."
– he is not impressed with my rendition,
possibly too midwestern –
but he seems content to listen
so we just enjoy the spring
in our own ways

because he knows that
the rains of april washed away the dust of march
and brought forth the trees and flowers
he has seen the wind blow through the fields
when the sun was high

and he has heard the nightingale near our camp
he has felt the restless urge to quest with me
so we, like countless others, go west
to heal our souls
and renew and refresh our beings
as ever and before
we each pay homage
as we can.

but i try to tell him

May

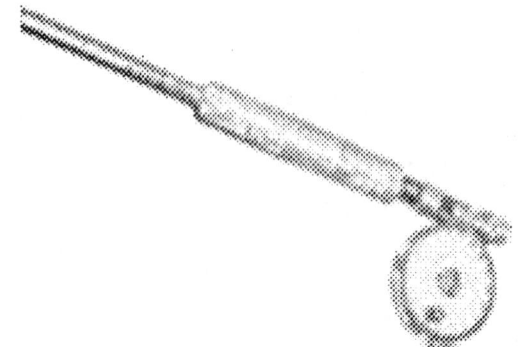

May 1

And now they all come out – turista of the waters, interested
more in the catching than the fishing. All manners of
beings, from soup to nuts, gather to pursue
– the quarry –
And all the flowers come out and all the newly borne
animals and all the schoold children
and the daze are gentle
and there is no challenge
and the springs and lakes and rivers clear
but –

there may be room for all,
if this catch and release stuff catches on
a trout or a bass is too valuable to be
"used just once" and
the key to survival on this planet
may just be
that everyone should just stop and go fishing
because I never met a human being who could
fish and worry at the same time
whether in a patch'ed jacket or orange jumpsuit
or an Abercrombie & Fitch field jacket.

And if the catching is so important,
then let the releasing be equally as important
– then it becomes more than just a matter
of a finny creature filling a niche in the human food chain
and the fishing, not the catching, can be the most important
gather while ye can
but get thee to a hatchery
so that there will be
enough promise of fish
for all.

May 2

Ah, technology . . .

We can put a man on the moon
but can we help a man catch a fish?
(if you just give him one, he has a meal, but if you . . .)
Sure.
Break that code and reveal the answers
It can and will be done.
I have benefitted from the march of science
Have you?
Then dont decry a man who fishes for other than
a sacred fish
All God's creatures got divinity
and deserve respect
Can you say LESS of humanity?
Then enjoy the democracy of fishing
A 22 lb. 5 oz. bass, if she now swims, and it is likely,
does not deign to peruse the pedigree of the potential
      world record holder.
The catcher matters not to the catchee.
So enjoy and respect codes broken or followed
Treat ALL with dignity
because it is found between the lines.

May 3

"Bust 'at hawg – if yew aint catchin, yew aint fishin"
quit droppin yr g's; you sound like a good ol boy
but yr listenin to th wurds, steada th tawlk
put g's where ya kin, don't dropg themg forg affectg
"Nowsk yousk soundsk likesk popeyesk"
I yam what I yam.

Then read of this fish and be forever in awe:

Micropterus salmoides
isn't as picky as some regarding the water;
ponds are as good as perrier
will take a dry fly, or worm, or a spinner bait or a mouse
but wont be foold twice

Man-made flood-control projects decimate trout streams
but make new homes for the bigmouth
so, enjoy, if it must come to pass,
the fishing of a reservoir.
and apply standards to thyself
rather than to another

oh, just fish once for Bertha and find out
that it is fun
and that it can be art
and that, if viewed from the wrong perspective,
a trout is rather a simple creature
who is an opportunist
and easily discouraged
by a change in temperature
or in the pH of the water

and who seems to have a fondness
for corn and marshmallow and garlic
for whatever reason –
but, if treated with respect . . .
will reward the seeker
with a vision into the magic
whether revealed by translucence
or technology

Be not a snob – I once found reason to live in a bass
– but that is a tale for the fall.

May 4

however
we have computerized fishing
encoded with the DNA is a digital code proscribing that
the fish will bite the patterns scheduled by
the fisherman's almanac
a tiny chip controls the process
and if you don't want to catch fish

just use the wrong fly
isnt this amazing?

i once read of a fisherman's dream in which he had died and gone to heaven
or so he thought
because he was on a beautiful stream
with a long rod
and the sky water trees sun
were perfect
and when he cast the first time he caught a five-pound trout
and thought he was in heaven
and the second cast brought an identical trout
and he thought he was in heaven
and the third and the fourth on so on brought the same results
and
with a sharp intake of breath
he knew . . .

even though the unravelling of mystery is a worthy quest
giving reason to live and learn
think of a world with no mystery left
and try to leave some of the magic alone
some erroneous thought patterns should not be debunked
at least, not now
created mysteries are less enchanting than those just appearing
in nature and in the human soul
and what would happen to curiosity
if the answers were already known

cant mystery just be appreciated, holmes
and the unravelling the thing
rather than the answer
of course,
eliminate the impossible
and keep the improbable

and that's the truth, however unlikely

May 5

I once took a course in quantitative philosophy
there was only one question on the final:
How many angels can dance on the head of a pin: count them
(the correct answer should be added to your notes,
      and turn in your pins with your paper)
– I gave the answer that I knew the professor wanted,
      even though I knew there were 47
less
than the prof. thought – some of them had gone fishing.
some of them just acted like they could dance too.

I thought the more important issue was:
– how many angels need to dance on the head of a pin –
isn't that sort of a mundane pursuit
rather trivial
is there a lot of down-time in the angel business these days
but in all fairness I know
that there is at least one guardian angel
who has guided my steps over mossy slick stream bottoms
and up rocky mountain peaks
and through treacherous valleys

i have kept this angel busy
as i pursued all the angles
looking for another way of looking
and sometimes wearing blinders
or at least stumbling
and never knowing
and never seeming to learn

but wondering
how many anglers can dance on the head of a pin
depends on the waters

and the current
and the rocks
and the size of the boots

and where in my map of america
any particular pin might be stuck
and there are more and more every day

May 6

THE THEORY OF RELATIVELY

you know –
the one that

gave us back the center of the universe

how does that work, you ask

                                                    well.

Once upon a time
        rulers (who decided these things)
        accepted the theory as fact
        THAT the
Evidently
Arable
Residential
Terrestriation
Here

        was the center of ever-thing

universe included.

(till Galileo,
but they got him to stay quite quiet on the matter)
THEN: word got out
and accepted one idea to the exception of others:

(our planet was not the center of the spheres)

AND THEN: some einstein came along and said that it all
depends upon where you are and when you are and probably
on who you are;
which is pretty good thinking
(relatively speaking, of course)
and it does put YOU at the center of things – doesn't it?
    (depends entirely upon your family – doesn't it?)
and, all things considered
    nepotism beats being on the dole roll

May 7

Does your family fish?
I'm sure at least one does.
It rather depends on who your family is.
Doesn't it?
I mean, if you are one of the Waltons,
Well . . .
But
If not then maybe it's your Uncle Bob
Who fishes.
I think everybody has an Uncle Bob
Mine doesn't fish, but I do.
He could, though –
Those qualities that make for a fisher
Are in him, but manifest in other ways –
He fishes for data.
And for those qualities in human beings
That make them what they could be
Instead of what they sometimes are.
He knows, as does the fisherpoet,
That boundaries are to be broken
Whether national or personal
And that there is good everywhere.
He fishes for lives and makes them rhyme
And for the spark in an eagle or a river.

Everyone should have an Uncle Bob,
Even if he doesn't fish.

May 8

progress happens
in funny ways . . .
some of my predecessors came from
detroit:
germanic mechanistics,
and yet
with a little scots-irish.
the other side of the family:
emigrant arkansawyers,
germanic agrarians
with a little scots-irish;
going back a ways –
most trace their ancestors to
immigrant aspirants . . .
mine, i think,
were invited to leave –
something about
unpopular ideas;
but various cousins
managed to bring
strains of brown trouts –
not a bad idea,
all things considered
progeny and progeny
meet at the spring branch.

May 9

i once thought
i would like to live in another time –
when life was, perhaps, simpler.
until i had a toothache.
i dont think whiskey and pliers

were a simpler cure than
a visit to my local dentist.
i once thought
i would like to live in another place –
where it does not get cold
until i went south
and found that
climes without winter
dont support trout
i had fun but . . .
couldn't feel at home.
i once thought
i would like to be someone else –
until i watched others walk
in their own moccasins
struggling with various problems
my own, somehow, did not seem so bad.
acceptance of reality is knowing:
    who
    where
    when
    you are
the nature of reality seems to be
    the reality of nature
i am content
    i am home
my son's roots are mine
    je ne sais quoi?

May 10

and yet still i wandered at times
seeking new experience over the horizon
on a quest for variations of the theme
but within the parameters of my dreams

waters flowing from mountains to seas
offered more chances to fish for trouts

with different trees in the foreground
or a different dialect of view

the search was, of course, a circle
leading me to my roots
how could i have known
but how fortunate i did not

i dont mean to say that i live by chance
but i do, if you know what i mean
opportunity springs from problems
unanticipated but necessary

no pain – no . . .
well, you know
life can be a cliche

or a truism

there is a difference.

May 11

i rigged the flyrod with a
grey nondescript
and double-haul cast to a lie
on a western river

catch-and-release
was my intent
but fishing was my need
salvation

a deer drank from the river
oblivious or perhaps disdainful
of my presence
quenched soundlessly leaving
the seven per-cent grade of the river road

made getting here easier
than leaving
on some days gravity works harder

i cast and watched
sat on a boulder for lunch
read in the sun
fished some more

some trout came to me
brooks and browns
but from downstream, not up
obviously misunderstanding the rules

i altered my cast to accommodate
until i melded with the cycle
the earth moved till the sun set and i left
quenched soundlessly leaving

May 12

do you know what a "mark" is?
back in the old days
some guys went west on the train
to denver and in the station
there was a barbershop with a sign:
  Haircut
  $.50
some sat down to have one
it was a bargain
the clipman turned the chair as he cut
and by the time it went around the sign read:
  Haircut
  $5.00
if the guy didn't squawk
then he would be marked by the clipman
with an inverted "v" notch
cut into the back of his hair –

other clipmen would see this and know;
and that's how a "mark" was spotted
by the conmen of denver in the old days
nowadays, it is easier to spot a "mark"
all a clipman has to do is promise
        The first one's free
or
        I can increase spending and lower taxes
or
        You can't win if you don't play
or
        (those three little words)
or
        It was owned by a little old lady who . . .
or
        almost anything, no matter how unbelievable
and the marks will run over each other to seek him out

trout and rivers make no such promises of bargains
        nor do i

May 13

Once't,
        i went bass fishing
        in a western pond
        i caught a bunch

Twice't,
        i went north
        to fish in boundary waters
        i caught toothy fishes

Thrice't
        i fished from boats
        in southern swamps
        where reptilian critters watched

Four times
    i tried to go east
    seeking the roots of tradition
    by going fishing

    initially and finally
    i found it
    in the center
    among the simple things
    of my youth

    it is not where but how we are
    that makes the difference
    do i make myself clear?

May 14

i pack my graphite rod into the nylon casing
the space-age plastics contribute to the lightness of my gear
how miraculous that these things can be created from
    elements
of course we have more elements now
the periodic table has grown some since the days of
    earth air water fire
which explains why there were no plastics
    during the renaissance

and yet, once i have packed this featherweight equipage
i head for the eternal wildness
to fish for primitive creatures little affected by
    technological change
except, perhaps, in the surplus of industry
ejected into the watershed
and the sulphurous wastes forming acid rain

but enough of this
i wont climb onto my soapbox here

surely you are aware of this and DOING someTHING
by now . . .

so, i want to go fishing to get away from it all
altho i take some with me
isnt that the best way –
to keep the finest and
jettison the problems?

i load the gear into the jeep
and go with the radio on (sometimes)
from my nylon tent,
having eaten freeze-dried foods
cooked over propane
as i drift to sleep
i listen to coyote and nightingale
and know the feeling of eternity

May 15

ANGLATOR: Hello.
SPORTSTOR: Hey!
ANGLATOR: Beautiful day.
SPORTSTOR: Yes. Catching any?
ANGLATOR: Some. Got a nice one earlier.
SPORTSTOR: Really? How good?
ANGLATOR: Oh, it was a brown of about eighteen inches. I got him on a dry at the tail of that pool under the bridge. It was tricky to keep him out of the pilings but I managed to ease him out. Released him in good shape and then caught some smaller rainbows and brookies.
METAPHOR: Greetings.
ANGLATOR: Hello.
SPORTSTOR: Hey!
METAPHOR: Good day for fishing, eh?
ANGLATOR: Beautiful day.
METAPHOR: How's fishing?

ANGLATOR: Not bad – got one good one earlier and some smaller fish since.
METAPHOR: How good was the good one?
ANGLATOR: Oh, it was a brown of about eighteen inches. I got him on a dry at the tail of that pool under the bridge. It was tricky to keep him out of the pilings but I managed to ease him out. Released him in good shape and then caught some smaller rainbows and brookies.
SPORTSTOR: You like upstream or down?
METAPHOR: I'm fishing dry, so up is probably better today, but I could change to a nymph and go down.
SPORTSTOR: Well, I already have a nymph tied on, so why don't I head down and you up?
METAPHOR: Sounds good.
ANGLATOR: Beautiful day for fishing.
SPORTSTOR: Yes!
METAPHOR: The quest for the sublime is embodied in those elements of nature symbolizing the metaphysical, yet functioning as literal parts of a microcosm of the universe as a whole. The individual contemplative aspect of engaging in an activity engenders ethereal images pertaining to the relationship of man to his world and of nature to time. I find that as I immerse myself in the waters of life that these elements manifest themselves in my being, both as immediate restorative and as paradigm directing individual perspective. Would you agree?
ANGLATOR: . . .
SPORTSTOR: . . .
ANGLATOR: I think I'll call it a day.
SPORTSTOR: Me too.

May 16

i sit facing the computer thinking how universal the experiences of the ages are. i may have freedom of speech but the computer still limits me to an eight character filename. so maybe i am being a little tongue-in-cheek but really the essence of these things is the same. as i sit here immunized against various diseases and with the thermostat controlling the interior weather the computer obeys my commands and the jeep stands patiently awaiting orders. i have at my disposal information in the form of books disks online services cable phone mail et cetera. although my last boat had but a simple sonar unit i could have installed several types of screened readout printout beeping devices enlightening me as to the mysteries of the deep and of the size profile and depth of the denizens as well as the probable lure to use. some forms of artificial intelligence can write poetry so i hear. but there are some things that need to be done in a simpler fashion. so i turn off the computer – it says goodbye to me – and go outside to the pile of next winter's wood. from behind it i grasp the gunwale of the aluminum john boat and drag it to the jeep and lift it to the luggage carrier where i tie it down. everything else is already waiting in the jeep. at the sound of the boat being moved the red setter comes from the woods and dances by the jeep. after a short drive on muddied gravel roads i come to a low-water bridge and pull off. gear is stowed and an electric motor is fitted to the transom and connected to a 12-volt battery. the red setter takes his place in the prow. as i move up the stream avoiding the gravel bars i note newfallen trees in the stream – spots i will want to fish on my drift back down. when i have gone far enough up the stream i cut the motor and pick up the fly rod. it is sized for this stream and already has a green spongy rubber-legged spider attached to it. my first cast is awkward. the spider lands in weeds and i flip the line backwards to begin a new cast. the weight-forward tapered line offers better control and as my judgement improves the second cast is on target launching the spider to the edge of the reeds. i let it sink in and then begin the retrieve. the sudden tug indicates bluegill and i set the hook. the afternoon passes pleasantly enjoying the fishing the company and the relaxing drift. we let the current carry us that way until we return to the bridge having caught and released a variety of fishes. perspective in hand we return to the cabin.

May 17

words wirds werds whirreds wurds
the fisherpoet has to choose
and yet not only or but nor
the meanings can diverge
or converge
and the irony (relatively speaking, of course)
is that divergent speaking leads to convergence
and verse visa
the bottom line (yuppily) is
simply completion
or beginning, if you would have it that way

Burt, thou never whirred
but cycled cross-country
and founded your own meanings
as you wend
your way
but within a larger sphere
neverending
if you would have it that way

Bullfinch, i say
fableous meanings are aparent in nature
and there are know knew ways under the son
but only gnu weighs of looking
good
as anywon
who nose

yule sea
i'll just take a cheese and egg Hamlet
with a little Bacon on the side
and contemplate the misstirry
of Poetree
Zounds! good to me

After all, a good play
is worth a thousand pictures
is worth a thousand
whurds wirrds juerdes hwurds words

May 18

Everybody sing!
    I got a dog his name is Rex
    (strum a G, strum a G)
    Ain't too bright but he knows how to fetch . . .
    (strum a G, strum a C,D,G)

Don't know that one? Try this one:
    I once loved a girl from the country
    (strum A minor)
    Her kisses were sweeter than honey . . .
    (strum F)
You're kidding – you never heard that one? Well, then:
    The old fiddle waits on the shelf
    (strum D and C and A)
    But the old fiddler has gone . . .
    (strum D, D, and A)

Come on! Where have you been?
Here. You take the guitar and you pick the song.
It doesn't matter what we sing
    as long as we sing.
This here campfire ain't the only thing that can warm us.
No, I don't know that one, but teach it to me.
It'll be better if we share than if we each sing our own.

There you go – I can sing that one.
Hey! That's pretty good.
Let's try a little harmony on the chorus.
That's a good one.
Let's sing a couple more and then turn in.
We want to be on the spring branch early
       for the best fishing.

May 19

How would you like to celebrate this day?
Did you think i would ever forget?

I forget almost nothing
except for names of course
and times of course
and whatever it was i was supposed to do
of course

but
i do remember
and again i ask
How would you like to celebrate this day?

I know how i would like to spend it –
walk with me along the spring branch
and share
the feelings and sights and timelessness of
the flow

and i will share with you the secrets
of the rocks and trees and water
and you will understand

and know that i am a simple fisherpoet
who sees in the elemental surroundings
those things which make sense
of all we do

and which bring peace and a sense of fulfillment
from being not an observer
but in the cycle

so walk with me and we will fish together
and maybe the best thing i can do
is to share this with you

How would you like to celebrate this day?

let yourself try this and see
and if it speaks to you
then celebrate all days as this one

May 20

Sometimes I go fishing for trout
Sometimes I don't –
I fish for other things

Sometimes when I go fishing for trout
I am fishing for other things
I can't not fish –

I was always told
That there are three kinds of people
And that I would have to choose my role.

Some watch what happens –
Some make things happen –
Some wonder what happened.

When it looks as though I am watching,
I am quite possibly doing something else
You just never know.

I may be observing, which is more than watching;
I may be planning or remembering.

But I am never not fishing.

I saw a sign once that said:
"No Fishing!"
You have probably seen one.

Well, on the surface I wasn't but
Down deep – well . . .
You know.

Twixt the womb, the grave, and the quest for the sublime
I fish and write my pome, oft in rime –
So much to fish for; so little time.

May 21

Anyone ever try to sell you the Brooklyn Bridge?
    Funny – it's been sold by more than the number
        who've owned it,
And it's not always a rip.
    That depends upon who or why the selling –
But mainly upon who profits from the venture.

All that glitters . . .
    Well, you know –
But some IS gold,
    Not all, but some.

I've heard and read of a few Bridge salesmen
    Who were not trying to get rich.
All things considered – they did not profit as much
    As those who bought –
But they still did not take a loss.

Don't misunderstand –
    It was still not a gift.
The gift had already been bestowed
    Upon the seller.

In my case – I don't know for sure
>> I have a bridge to sell you, just a small bridge.
Let's us hope that we can both profit from the deal;
>> Equitability suits me.

May 22

What kind of world do you live in?

It could be a primitive world
>> with dangers abounding.
Or a world of the dark ages
>> which only seem so after the fact
You could aspire to a renaissance world
>> with aspirations in all directions
Maybe you live in a transcendental world
>> or a romantic world.
Possibly you reside in a victorian world
>> guarding your ankles so carefully
If you live in a modern world
>> you may now be old-fashioned
You may find yourself being post-modern
>> but still not contemporary
And even the idea of being just that
>> will soon be dated.
What kind of world do you live in?

Perhaps any world is not a place
>> but rather an attitude
Offering a perspective on time
>> and on thought
Any Einstein could figure out
>> that $e=mc^2$
But who in science would agree
>> that $w=t$
That is – that the world
>> equals the times
How about $a=t=w$,

        involving attitude?
I wonder – I ponder this
    I cannot understand that
people believe w=p
        place just doesn't cover it.

What kind of world do you live in?

I live in a world where attitudes begets DOING

DOING begets BEING begets SEEING begets KNOWING.

I have no formula for this equation, but i have found
        my particular answer.

May 23

by now you may have assumed
at least, i assume you have
that progress does not equal progression
altho the two can be related
technology is not necessarily a part of one
but is inextricably inherent in the other
so
it depends upon what is sought
and i prefer progression
the fish my son catches
are the issue of fish i caught years ago
which were issue of my father's catches
this is by no means progress, but . . .
the reliability of the situation
lends itself more to the development of values
than the situational ethics of chip-directed intellect

ask any politician his first priority
and if honest (relatively speaking, of course)
he (or s/he, to be politically correct) will say:
"getting re-elected"

after all, that is the closest situational condition
to being elect
but is progress really achieved in this manner?

ask me about progress and i will tell you
that it is a matter of adapting technology
to essential values –
not
the exchange of the old for the new
or the plain for the glittery

until that comes to pass
i will believe in progression
as the inevitable goal
of worthwhile life

May 24

and yet
how marvelous the mind of man
to conceive
> the wheel
> the electric light
> the internal combustion engine
> vaccines
> waves carrying music invisibly through the air
> microwave ovens
> computer chips
> lasers
> and . . . and . . . and . . .

how fortunate that we no longer burn people at the stake
who conceive the inconceivable

my life is not hampered by invention
but by misapplication
by using power to crush rather than build
or control to diminish others for personal gain

the lifes of humankind no longer need end in tragedy
altho it is nature's way
that the life of any and every wild animal
must end tragically and in suffering
we can extend life
but at the same time
must dedicate energy to expanding the quality of life
within our stewardship

May 25

i just flew in from heathrow and
boy, are my arms tired.
wait, you misunderstand – i dont mean it as a bad joke
i had to carry multi-suitcases for miles through a complex
so, wait to hear the entire tale before divining my intent

how many [fill in your own]
does it take to change a light bulb?
it depends
it only took one edison
to change it into a reality

i went to the doctor the other day
and said, "Hey, Doc – it hurts when [whatever]"
and he (or she) said:
"Then don't do that anymore."
so i paid

none of this matters except that the joke may be that this is not funny
intent equals content
and any punch line is only funny if
the listener is immune to the punch.

May 26

so me and the red setter went fishing

he has a good sense of humor
but knows no jokes
he doesn't need them to create good mood
and he is playful without guilt
which is something i try to learn from

we fish together on the spring branch
or on a new river
the fishing, catching, and doing
matter less than the shared being
we catch each other's mood

other companions often join us
but we willingly share and enjoy
the setter's humor is contagious and his energy inspiring
he sets the example and checks whether we follow

if i could distill the essence of his mood
bottle it and carry it with me
i would share it with anyone

the best i can do is to collect the images
and sort through them for nuggets

and share them with you in this pome.

May 27

some criticize technology
saying life would be better if simpler
i don't argue vehemently
but
i don't see them refuse to use modernity
for the most part
a few, of course, do this
most just yammer about
        the good old days
after sifting the experience,

mentally removing
    those little boulders in the road
i take the good and the bad from the past
    and
    from
    technology

without the progression
so much and so many would not exist
i choose the best and leave the rest
i never whine about what is
because everything that ever was
has a good side
for
somebody

May 28

i know devout pagans
who worship trees
they offer me logic
to open my eyes
beyond belief

a tree, they say, gives
wood for
    fire, both heating and cooking
    houses and shelters
    tools
    weapons and sports
    beds, chairs and tables
    musical instruments
    toothpicks
    shelves to hold things
    bridges
    wagons
    toys
    desks

railroad ties
canes and crutches
splints
picture frames
stairs
candlestick holders
doors
dashboards
boxes
railings
baskets
– even the pages of this very book –

all manner of neccessities and luxuries
and what has your god done for you lately?

what can i say?
all i can do is counter with another question –
where did your tree come from?

May 29

don't get me wrong!
i'm not here to alter your belief in any way –
just your perception

even that is not through persuasion
but through showing you some things

like the way a stream works
bugs and all
and how a trout fits into a modern existence
primitive habits and all

like where you can go
to see what is
in order to appreciate
        nature

bloody in tooth and fang
        and all

my own beliefs are what i was exposed to
not what i was told
i have seen much and done much
i have learned to understand and accept
beyond appearances

when i read or hear a definition
i marvel at the diversity of meaning
and refine define
to relevance
so that my pack is not too heavy
but so that i have what i need
modernity has (relatively speaking, of course)
made that possible
through the wonders of
        technology
          ah!

May 30

so i packed all my gear and headed west
i crossed
        forests
        prairies
        high plains
        mountains
        deserts
i looked for that
        distillation of experience that waits to be discovered
but will never come to the pilgrim

i stopped at truckstops for coffee and conversation
        finding philosophy and life working hand in hand
we talked fishing, of course
but with few words

because we knew
    had been there
    had seen it
    had done it
    had enjoyed it
    had suffered the pain
    had lapped up the glory
but most of all
    were going
    (that is, doing and being)

so i had another cup for it was early
there were miles and miles to go
the setter tethered to a tree
    for his own good
rankled and faunched
as i had done
    so we left the interstate
not sure, but looking.

May 31

in the old days –
i would not have had time to fish for much
other than sustenance
which is really what i do now
but differently

i could not have carried books with
    they were prohibitively expensive then
    as life without them is now
i would never have gone fishing with
    Montaigne
    Mark Twain
    McClane
    McGuane
but now i do

things cost less
there are more things
some things are good
some things are bad
(relatively speaking, of course)

i can go or stay
if i pay the price
what counts is
        dedication
        perspective
        openness
        awareness

i leave room in my attache for
        a book
        a pack rod
        some leaders
        a box of Adamses
        a laptop computer
and a change of socks and underwear.

June

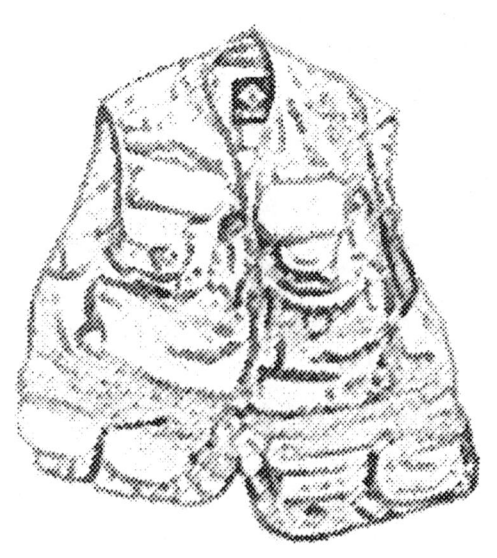

June 1

Just as the summer hits its stride
Unilateral forces join
Near the
Equator

Summery thoughts fill
Philosophical
Observations
Objectively
Negating

Marry thee at this time
Own that which becomes a family man
Or
Neutralize those instincts forevermore

Carry with pride the
Rod
Of
One or the other of those who live in the
Now

Take up a pencil
Uncase the long rod
Need only those things you have
Evermore

June 2

i cast the fly, a white grub-like nymph
into the upper reaches of the pool
it sank and drifted with the current
tumbling naturally but at the wrong depth
lead was added and another cast made
still at the wrong depth, it needed more impetus
to reach the lie

rather than add more lead
which already whistled menacingly past my ear
i cast further upstream for a longer drift
it fell into the foodstream and headed for the lie
i could see the flash in the current
as the trout turned
and the refracted sunlight reflected the rainbow
my fly disappeared and i struck
initially feeling the throbbing of life
then the fish strategized and ran upstream
a good maneuver for me but not for the trout
because the current worked with me
then the trout turned and ran down
creating slack
i coiled line furiously but in careful coils
because soon the current would not be in my favor
sure enough, i found myself having to work for leverage
the only thing to do was to move myself downstream
or else fight the trout and the current and the length of line
so i did
and finally turned the fish back upstream
then the trout dove and i had to put on pressure
then the trout leaped and i had to give line
ultimately, the balance worked in my favor
the trout came to the net
some are destined for release
and yet
some are not
this trout found its way to an almondine bed
in my iron skillet
the predator must husband the prey
but the responsibility must be met
and the cycles fulfilled with awareness
and it was good

June 3

the spring branch runs clear in summer

after the rains and snowmelt
have enriched it with foreign molecules
the surrounding forests wear greened robes
of growth life and health
midst fishing i pause to take this in
      because
where a trout is caught is integral
to the trout itself

this is no ancient wisdom – it had to be learned
once (this is in the books)
an individualistic thinker sought to have trout near
he was willing to work for the privilege
but that is not enough
he loaded up barrels of them
on a covered wagon
he made the grueling trip from back east
all the way to Missouri
and released his charge into a river
thinking that he would be planting seed
for the future –
imagine his glorified feelings at his accomplishment
never realizing that fish, of necessity, have standards
and cannot survive where conditions are not right
they need clear cold oxygenated water
and a good habitat
imagine his feeling of "a job well done"
when he dumped the last barrel
into the Mississippi River
where the trout could not last a day
ah, well –
it took me some time to learn this about myself
and i had more sources of information

June 4

the fisherpoet casts the line
but pulls up short

to allow the line to fall to the surface
imbued with snake-like curves
slack to reduce the effect of current
the leader is treated to sink into the film
rather than to lie on top
the fly appears to danse freely, unattached
from below, what matters is silhouette

is it a trick or a convention to do this?
the trout enters the zone of free accord
striking the fly – begins the danse royale
it is played out
the fisherpoet cradles the trout gently in one hand
until it is rested
and can breathe easily
and moves back into the current
when it chooses

a trout held gently will not struggle
peace comes upon it for a moment
and it allows calm observation
before release
does it realize that it is being worshipped
as a representative of life –
does it allow this moment to be
a peaceful symbolic moment
of love respect and tenderness?

June 5

sometimes i remember huck finn
i take the cane pole to the creek and fish for
whatever i find
on a bright summer's day
there is no better fun than to watch
a red and white bobber ploong
under the surface
and feel the thrumping as

a brightly colored bluegill
cuts circles in the water
on a lazy day
other times i
use sophisticated gear
i cast a dry irrestistable toward a log
perhaps to a nest
i hear a ploonk as a green sunfish
smacks the fly
it won't leap, as such
but – when it runs to the end of the line
sometimes the impetus will carry it
straight up into the air
do you suppose that He
was particular about what he fished for?
or did he relish the simple joy
of having cast without prejudice
and catching
what was there to be caught?

June 6

my son
using neither fly rod nor cane pole
prefers butterfly net or bare hands
and seeks his own
i dip the styrofoam cooler into the creek
to fill it with water
i set it next to the low-water bridge
so that he can collect his catch
soon the cooler abounds
with crayfish, tadpoles, snails, darters,
frogs, and fish –
they inhabit this domain for a time
until he deigns to release them
none the worse for wear
at times i leave the rod cased and join
in the barefooted pursuit

he smiles at the adventure
ignoring the mud and moss
on his feet and hands
this is like . . .
this is the kind of experience that . . .
. . .
if you have never done this –
there is no way to describe it
in a way that you can understand
you just have to do it –
soon.

June 7

One year, we trekked to the northlands
a canoe was launched on a pristine lake
the child was a napping babe in the canoe
with a sweatshirt for a sun-umbrella
the canoe drifted into a cove
which was filled with waterlilies and logs
surrounded by marsh grass
painted turtles sunned on logs
observing us as we them
until we drifted too close and they dove
on an island in the cove
we spotted the shape of a nest
really more of a cluttering of grass
we drifted closer
until the form of a mama loon took shape
on her nest with young
she refused to be intimidated
by our appearance
but seemed to take heart in the awareness
that we only drifted so close
before dipping a paddle and backing out
quietly
the boy and the loon babes
rested peacefully throughout

knowing they were cared for.

June 8

driving across oklahoma
i saw a bumper sticker
it gave me thought
but not for the thought contained

it was not witted
nor punned
it neither complained
nor pronounced

it was a nice thought
i guess
but didnt tell me anything new
or even anything at all

it was a gentle reminder
to do that
which should be done
often

what did it say?
you ask
only this:
take a kid fishing

but i had to wonder –
who needed
to be reminded of this
who didnt know?

the answer was
people whose kids wear t-shirts
with a message that
they somehow think humorous:

my parents went
somewhere
and all i got
was this lousy t-shirt.

try this:
let a kid take you fishing
and try to follow the good example
set for you.

June 9

did you ever see
a chucklehead?technically
it is a sculpin inhabiting the
fringes of cold clearwater creeks
it often shares waters with trout
and is often forage for big browns
it is hard to describe – its head is too big
the coloring is unlimited but mottled
its brown or green tones are filled with blues and reds and blacks
it has a voracious appetite
and sometimes takes a fly
intended for a trout
though it is never large
enough to give a fight
the pectoral fins are
like vertical wings
and rather fan-like
see-through and
very varicolored
the boy tries
to catch one
gently with
his hands
but they
are fast
so he
uses
a fly
and
c
a
t
c
h
e
s
o
n
e

June 10

METAPHOR: There is more to this fishing stuff than meats the aye.
ANGLATOR: You are beginning to understand – I think.
METAPHOR: I am working my way toward a realization.
ANGLATOR: That remains to be scene – hoo, hooo!
METAPHOR: What? But I'm the one who . . .
ANGLATOR: Relax – I can learn too.
METAPHOR: Ahh. Once again you have shown me something and in a way that I can not help but see. Will it always be this way – will I have to keep learning forever and ever?
ANGLATOR: If you are lucky. If you are observant. If you never believe that you have learned it all.
METAPHOR: But will I be able to say that I have accomplished something along the way?
ANGLATOR: Yes. You will have learned the art of fysshing with an angle (metaphorically speaking, of course).
METAPHOR: And then?
ANGLATOR: And then.
SPORTSTOR: It is a beautiful summer's day. The mayflies are hovering in clouds above the stream.
Trout are rising. Birds are singing. Bells are ringing (for me and my gal). The adventure awaits us. Let us quit this talk and go fishing. Now if not sooner.
ANGLATOR: He speaks wisely. Let us go to the spring branch. The fisherpoet has already been there and has moved on up. We shall follow his example.
METAPHOR: I get it!
ANGLATOR: Yes.
SPORTSTOR: Let's go!

June 11

now is not a time for counting
anything
DOING and BEING
take precedence

summer warmth provides
all necessary shelter
lay by the spring branch
and rest when you tire

stay out there
for your revelations
await you
where sought

if you are winning
now is the time to keep on
later
you can count

if you think you are not
then ask me
i will tell you
you are

just to be here
is part of winning
it is the main part
here – you can not lose.

June 12

sloganize yourself –
fecundity is imperfidious

what you seek is there
have no doubt
i have been to the spring branch
many times

each time is new but
each time is the same

all things are different but
everything is the same

i am different but
i am the same

June 13

i fish for many fishes in the spring branch
        yet i fish other places for other fishes
my approach is different depending –
        the results, however, are similar

my catch has little and everything
        to do with fishes
my pome has tried to tell this
        but you understand

summer is not the limiting factor
        in this activity
it is mainly the enaction
        of the symbolic ceremony

the true process is more like a seed
        lying seemingly dormant
yet ascending from the earth
        coming to fruition in its time

in my seed days i
        sat by a fire tying flies

i write and the setter sleeps
        the tackle rests in its place
in my shoot days i fidgeted
        and the setter runs
we watch the days until
        the kalends of march

my budding was and is tentative action
        forever young and life-ful
anticipation and realization
        the quest begins

flowering occurs throughout summer
        and yet
it is not the complete culmination
        of the cycle

i am but yet not halfway through
        there is more to be done
and more to understand
        before the cycle completes.

June 14

but does the lack of

    experience

mean a lessening of skill?

isupposethatinsomecasesitcould

    but
it also carries the idea of

    enthusiastic amateurism

and, after all –
the root of that word is *amat*, as
> *amore*

altho the good ol boy who once knew the local creek
could once count on outfishing the city slicker,
it has now been noted that:
an urban fisher can employ his urbanity
knowing more just the flow of the waters.
he will not fish as often but more knowledgeably.
and so . . .

love makes up for experience

June 15

i have wondered why
>a license is needed:

to fish
to drive
(to drive from the back seat)
to hunt
to inspect a car
(or eggs)
or to practice medicine
or law
or plumbing
or even to take liberties in a poem
>yet

none is required to own a pet
oh, sure –
the pet must be licensed
but not the owner
how about that?
one needs a license to do things
but not to own another living thing
(forget about marriage licenses –
they do not carry privileges of

        ownership)
but the strangest of all to me
is that parenting has no requirements of
        licensing
isn't the stewardship of another human being
important enough to necessitate at least
        minimum requirements?
well . . .
        i think so.

June 16

on a summer evening i sit in camp with the setter and watch the stars with the red setter. i wonder how many different things he hears than i do – crickets and whippoorwills thrum in the hidden and distantly a coyote calls for understanding. i hear these things and know what they mean to me, but what do they mean to the setter whose primal instincts lay closer to the surface than mine? i pause thinking that the instinct for comradeship has overcome all others and that he prefers to be with me in my camp than coursing with baying wolves. as you love me, red setter – as you love me. on other nights the air has carried sounds now unique but once indigenous: we camped near a pow-wow and listened in the night to the drums. no amount of televised offerings could prepare for feelings brought out by the actual sounds of the drums in the night coming from the direction of reflected fireglow in the distance. and yet they are mainly gone now through misplaced displaced sense of purpose. perhaps, although i realize it is now too late, our progenitors should have overcome some of their sense of purpose and just followed that most overwhelming of instincts: comradeship. if they had just come in from the night and sat by the fire they would have seen love and unity in operation. this the setter and i now know. and we can share the night sounds and food even though the implications are different and our purposes are different. neither he nor i claim ownership of the crickets or trees or even of the fire. our purposes diverge but our cycles intersect. our manifest destiny includes the idea that we should be and do, but the underlying principle is to share. this did have to be learned; in my misguided youth, i thought i owned the setter and enrolled him in an abeyance school. the director (of note) informed me that if this dog ever did anything i requested it would be because the dog wanted to do it and not because i ordered it. after i understood this, i never asked the red setter to do anything without good reason – and he did whatever i asked. i honored his requests in return. how much better it is to share being and doing. when we turn in the music of the woods carries us beyond the spheres and toward a new day of fishing, running, swimming, and creating pomes; i forget which of us did which.

June 17

the first cast of the morning falls short
if it is perfect
or too easy
it portunes later slovenliness
i mean: it is a bad sign
the first cast is a flex of arm and line
it must be made before the rest of the casts
an intentionally bad first cast is
        however
a bad sign too
i mean: it portunes later slovenliness
it should be good
        but not too perfect
after the first i consider the mechanics of the cast
the line should lift gracefully from the surface
excess water shaking free in a mist
the curve of the line should be in proportion
to the distance cast
the rod should be loaded with kinetic energy
but additional force will be exerted
power must be applied at the right moment

or it will fall short
it moves through a cycle and the timing must be right
the last curve must accelerate and move
      in a new direction
at last the entire line moves forward in space
but the cast is not done yet
the line must straighten out and
      suspend
briefly
before falling to the surface
a mere bit of reverse force at the right moment
causes the line to settle gracefully
in even curves
the leader sinks below the surface
and the fly begins its floating drift
unsuspectable toward the lie
the lure is the point of the cast.

June 18

you know . . .
fishing downstream is a different THING
than fishing upstream
know why?
logistics. that's why
down
you meet the fish head on
but the current is to your back
if you hook a fish it too fights

up
the fish don't face you
the current shows them only the lure
and pushes them toward you
wading is harder but really safer

all too soon
i will be a warrior prince

floating downstream on a barge
with all my possessions
and quite possibly on fire
even trout and salmon comprehend this:
they fight for their lives heading up to spawn
only when they are done with their cycle
do they drift downward in death

June 19

the gestalt is important but
detail is everything
the leader is the finest point of connection
it determines whether a trout can be landed
where a fly falls
the realisticity of the lure
(thru its invisibility)
and the length of the cast

there are numerous formulae
for the "perfect" leader
one is that two thirds must be butt
and one third tippet
the heavier portion must be strong and straight
while the forward section must be flexible
strong beyond its apparent diameter
and near to invisible
lying just beneath the surface
with enough slack to prevent artificial drag

it may glow or carry an indicator
it may be knotless or connected
       by blood knots
it may fasten to the main line
through a nail knot, glue, or an eyelet
but the connection must be solid
its cost belies its importance
but it determines everything

think of this
the next time someone asks
if you have the qualities of
a good leader

June 20

if wishes were fishes then . . .
but they are not.
i seek not to escape through fishing
rather to engage

the fisherpoet enters the stream full of hope
dreams
memories
thought
experience (always lacking somewhat)
and (some say) luck

if this were truly an escape
then it would be to a perfect world
which none, of course, are but
this world comes as close as any i know

even though fishing may not solve
"the world's problems"
it enables me to cope
to put things in perspective
to BE and to DO
(relatively speaking, of course)

fishing fuels for life
and though an end in itself sometimes
it carries over to . . .
well – THINGS in general
my hopes are modest

it would be nice to catch fish
on a beautiful day
sharing the experience
with a good friend
who understands
but there are moments
when the only important wish
stems from the eternal mystery:
will my waders leak today?
i really hope not.

June 21

No solstice for the wicked; no solace for the angler
The extra minutes of sunlight simply mean more time
between the productive sunrise and sunset
unless, of course, the long daylight is interrupted
by the hatch

Clouds of olive mayflies complete the cycle begun with
birth
the year of nymph-larva-ness is over in a day
and another is sought to share the miracle of procreation
and their cycle completes its round and intersects
with the food chain

Of trout who have their own cycle to complete
altho this is not the epitome-epiphany of their own cycle
unless –
the drifting mayfly, looking like all the other drifting
mayflies
suddenly attaches to a jaw

Like a badge or medal
and if that minuta insecta
suddenly begins to direct the trout's movements
toward an animated and yet stationary being

toward which instinct directs to offer resistance

And when there is no place in the water where the thing can
        be gotten rid of
A wingless flight toward heaven ensues
suggesting freedom, but offering only a temporary releaving
        of the pressure
and then the gravity that brings all to earth takes hold
and alternate directions are sought

And all seems futile, except for the fact that
fecundity rules

June 22

and so it goes
one summer fishing trip after another
the greenage of the surroundings
makes pleasant the trek

the trout of this spring branch
or others
willingly participate in my adventure
or theirs

no serious obstacles block me
in my pursuit
i am
        lazy
        crazy
        hazy
        dazy
        mazy
        phasey

and why not?
it is summer

the red setter runs along the bank
sometimes in the stream
but he does not splash in the pools wherein i fish
i never taught him that
but he somehow knows

perhaps in the same way that he knew
that he could turn a door knob
and let himself out for a walk
i wonder if we were reversed-role partners
in an earlier life

June 23

much needs be accomplished in summer;
despite the vacation aspect if the season,
now is the time to DO THINGS that need
to BE done.

i have painted and mowed at times
i have planted and sown at times
now i appreciate the growing things
of the wild

no good reason exists to tame
wild plants
so i let them do what they do
and they return that respect

so what about those things that do
need to be done?
well – they are research
for everything

i had some good teachers
i think of them from time to time
one reminded me to

never let schooling get in the way of my education

another, with a wry grin
said that it can take a long time
to UNcover all the material
related to the subject

summer is a good time for that
or for other STUFF
why?
because that's what i do . . .
       gnnorrffgh!

June 24

It was a time to . . .
    i dont know
perhaps fulfill my place in the cycle of life and go into
partnership with a significant other who would one day
leave to fulfill another cycle
    but i didnt know that then
even if i had
i wouldnt have changed a thing or missed it for the world
who knows when donning a tuxedo and signing
    that piece of paper
that it may (more than half the time and rising) be a prelude
    or page one
to another piece of paper this time taking back all the
    promise of the first
Paul Harvey never told me and so i went ahead with it and
    wearever you go there you air
and you leave and you find out
that there was probably no reason
    for any of it but
it seemed right at the time and maybe it was and maybe its
just another reminder of how temporary everything can
really be and how all that can be truly lived is the moment

and so it can still be celebrated in a way even though it can
never be gone back to
as my ol buddy says:

> going back is like putting sour milk back in the
> refrigerator thinking it will be better
> the next time you take it out

the cycle has to go on and only a part can be revealed
        at a time
even though renewal and progression can sometimes
        crush the forest
to put up parking lots
and sometimes the only spaces left are marked
"handicapped"
and are empty anyways

> ah well what the hell
> i go fishing for life and
> the important thing is the fishing –
> not the catching

June 25

bib entry:

Shaffer, Tony. <u>Life</u>. Sedalia: Public Demesne, 1950.

I might have enjoyed a celebrated birth but
the Korean Wa- . . . police action broke out
MASH units proeceded anticipated movies
and television shows
to be yet further syndicated
and the concept of "a World at War"
was reduced to an action
and of policing at that

and when Johnny marched home

he had no idea that he had not fought in a war
and when he did not march home
he had no idea that he left a fatherless child
who would live through the days of
the Viet Nam Wa- . . . situation
and sometimes go to fight
and sometimes try to not
and be barred from bars
where vets of "real" wars
waxed about the horrors
of guns and bombs
not knowing of orange agents
and, too, my celebrated birth took a back seat
        to Autie Custer's last stand
in which Native Americans fought a true last stand
how do you say it – won the battle but lost the war?
and then I wonder what I am to do
fish the Yellowstone?
write a pome?
why was I born this day, temporally opposed
        to the celebration of Christ's day
and with no way to supersede or change any history
        except my own
and so I fish
and so I write
and so I play upon my guitar
        the theme from MASH
        and Custer's song –
one was "Garryowen"
the other was "Suicide is Painless"
but the distinction eludes me
except where i am concerned

June 26

what makes a place perfect?
not the place itself
because then it would be perfect

without our presence
no
what makes a place special
is what we do there
and how we feel there
how it is anticipated
remembered
and enjoyed

i have found such places
their qualities were
sometimes not apparent
upon first look
i had to let them approach me
in their own ways

and yet
sometimes
not very often
i have entered a place
and felt at home from the start
almost as though
i had been there before

maybe i have
or maybe someone else
has been there
and left something
in proportion to what
they gained
while they were there
i hope
to do the same.

June 27

ANGLATOR: Fish now; talk later.
SPORTSTOR: OK

***

ANGLATOR: I have one
SPORTSTOR: I see. It looks like a good one.
ANGLATOR: That it is, but then they all are.
SPORTSTOR: You catch only good fish?
ANGLATOR: That depends upon your definition of "good fish." All of the fish I catch are good, whether in size or heart or color or time.
SPORTSTOR: You mean you don't care what you catch?
ANGLATOR: No, not at all. But I do not believe any fish that can give such joy and beauty and meaning can be not a "good fish."
SPORTSTOR: Not even an ugly carp?
ANGLATOR: No, not even a carp can be a "bad fish."
SPORTSTOR: I do not understand your priorities.
ANGLATOR: Nor I yours, but give some time to consideration before becoming set in your ideas. You may find that there are some superseding perspectives.
SPORTSTOR: How will I know?
ANGLATOR: Just keep fishing.

***

METAPHOR: How fare you?
SPORTSTOR: Well – very well.
METAPHOR: Any good ones?
SPORTSTOR: All of them . . . I think.
ANGLATOR: Take your time.
METAPHOR: Well, I caught some little ones, but the big one seems to elude me. I think I will try from the other side of the stream. Maybe that is a better place.
SPORTSTOR: But . . .
ANGLATOR: All places are good places, but give it time if you want to understand.

SPORTSTOR: Oh . . . yes.
METAPHOR: Huh?
ANGLATOR: Just fish.
METAPHOR: Just fish?
SPORTSTOR: Just fish.

***

June 28

time moves so quickly on the spring branch
despite the sense of eternal renewal
my day scarcely begins before it is time to pack the gear
and return to the cabin

the paradox is that summer days, being the longest,
turn out to be the shortest.
we try to enjoy every minute, greedily savoring
every aspect of the experience
it is difficult to realize at the moments
of BEING and DOING that we are making memories
sometimes it seems as though we are just enjoying
another day in our own personal paradise

so the day ends much as it began:
the sun is upon the horizon
colored in pastels and neons
the temperature is lower and shadows longer

the fish rise to the newly abundant hatch
insecta circling transforming falling floating
and I match the hatch as best i can
(using an adams of reasonable size)

a trout takes and i play the fish gently
soon i land it and pause for a moment
to appreciate the rare beauty of this moment
and to store the details for another season.

June 29

but how can i fish for trout in missouri
when there are other places
with other scenery
with other adventures?

the high plains rivers of wyo
seem wilder than those of mo
and the mountain freshets of co
seem to offer more than so
(dakota that is)

i head west in my jeep
with my STUFF and the red setter
needing no more than essentials
just needing to be going
i fish the west – the rockies and high plains
snowmelt creeks and volcanic lakes
strangely though, what i find is not there
i suppose i brought it with me

i realize the need to slow down
but the drive is upon me
loading stuff and setter into jeep
we head off into the horizon.

June 30

a sense of ritual surrounds the setting up of a new camp
tents pans ropes pegs firefuels tackle
and all the rest of the et cetera
must be placed just so to make this into a home

the setter takes the opportunity to run
        and check out the woods
he will come back when he is ready
meantime i brew swedish coffee

in the aluminum pot
(forget about the eggshells – i percolate)
by the time the aroma has enticed me to rest,
the setter has returned

answering his request i remove burrs and sticktites
he curls in the shade by the tent for a nap
his way is to run full-tilt and then rest until
he is ready to go again

somehow that seems better than schedules i have attended
the clock seems to rule me in other places but here . . .
i eat when hungry and sleep when tired
there is no quota nor duty list
time moves differently and i follow the example of the setter
the cot is ready and i lay in the shade thinking of other camps
and dreamily anticipate the rising of the sun.

as the setter sleeps, his legs and nose twitch mightily
he probably dreams of other times and places
and relives memories in his way.
my feet probably lay still when i sleep
but i bet my smiles project unhindered
as i relive other days
in my own way.

July

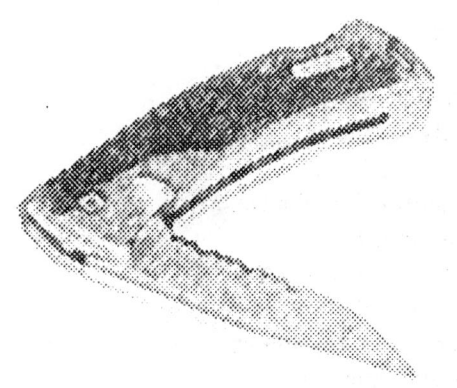

July 1

i stand on the edge of a flaming gorge
relocated to the american west
tho i know my roots
i feel
somehow
at home

i remember each mile of the way
but absorbing the treeswatermountainssky
i feel on another plane or planet

the creeksize river is green here traversing the
rockies dams and weirs and surviving
in spite of the power taken from it

the aloneness here is only
the absence of other people
and the comradery of the stream
keeps spirits
escalating

trouts abound
a larger fly asserts

i find what i seek in the waters
and try to return
and try to return what i have taken
and see so clearly now
that what is over my shoulder
differs so completely
from what i see ahead of me.

July 2

My father fished before the war
The big one

When the streams were wild and free
And he taught me the strength
Of a delicate fly rod.
My mother fished later
To share
We three formed a triumvirate
And communed in our way.
That is when I was told the stories
Of my family.
There were many and they did things
Some big, some small.
Undivided by the miles, but
As many families,
By attitude.
What I learned in that triangle
Is what I carry still –
It is one thing to be
Individualistic
And quite another to be
Independent.

July 3

I learned what I learned
    in that little triangle.
Do you know it?
    that geometric figure, i mean
It is the place formed by the intersecting
    of three circles – three cycles
Draw them
    you'll see it
If you draw more circles
    that space in the middle changes
Doesn't stay a triangle
    becomes something else
I was fortunate to be a part
    of the strongest possible structure
Diversity can be best appreciated

        from the security of invulnerability
It has always been so with me.
        for that i am grateful
Don't misunderstand me –
        i don't understate your strengths
I just mean that they come from
        a different foundation
Do what you do in your own way
        and find your strengths

July 4

I celebrate
by hiking
far from the maddening crowd
up up into the mountains
beyond the huge reservoir with its
lake and rainbow and brown trout
I follow the freshet from its mouth
to a series of beaver dams
forming small pools
containing rainbows
brooks cutts and browns
and I see not a soul all day
tho this is no more than a mile from the road
some pools contain many smaller trout
and one large one
it is here that chances would be best
for catching a huge brown
I hear not a sound except for those
generated in nature
none of the explosive renderings
of ancestral battles
but in the mountains, the word is the same
freedom waited here to be found
and I did.

July 5

camp is set.
the setter runs in the forest.
i load the fly rod with a colorful streamer –
casting toward the beaver dam,
i maintain a low profile in the scrub brush.
one after another, brookies compete for the fly.
when one takes i catch-and-release it
and move to a new pond for a while,
sometimes drifting the fly under an undercut,
sometimes catching a cutthroat trout,
sometimes just enjoying the scene
eventually i work my way to the source of the stream,
a volcanic crater ringed by lightningstruck trees.
the water here is so clear (gin, crystal, air, etc.)
that trout appear suspended but they disappear
when i cast to the lake
i settle upon a different method
one used by pacific northwest steelheaders
and load a shooting head onto the line
to cast amazing distances
the line sinks, carrying the fly to the depths
(an olive woolybugger, to be specific – tied it myself)
a slow retrieve induces a throbbing pull
and soon i am fast to a large rainbow.
this fish is short and stocky with a muscular tail
which propels him through the air and water
without seeming to recognize the difference.
and i can think of no place on earth
that i'd rather be at this moment
altho, in all honesty,
i really don't try very hard.
pace. *pace.*

July 6

ANGLATOR: Today is the day. We will fish further up the river until we find new stretches of water. These will be no better than the places we have already fished, but will offer different problems requiring different solutions. The current flow will be unlike it is in the pools and riffles you have already fished so your techniques must be altered to compensate. It is a way to see whether you know fishing well or whether you know the river well. To fish well, you must learn to read the river and all of its changes. Let us go up and learn.

SPORTSTOR: Good. I have grown tired of fishing this same area over and over. I look forward to seeing new things.

METAPHOR: I like to look at the same things differently, as you well know. If I were to say that something different is something different, would I confuse you?

ANGLATOR: You never confuse – you usually puzzle. We will see what happens when we get there.

SPORTSTOR: How much further must we walk? I am carrying all the food and drink in addition to my tackle. If we do not get there soon, I must stop for a rest.

ANGLATOR: Arrest your whining then and keep walking. We look for new places and must travel further than the worn path.

SPORTSTOR: I am sorry, but I am carrying the supplies for all three of us. Would one of you like to help? I could be persuaded to share this character-building carrying.

ANGLATOR: Let us stop for a moment and take a drink.

SPORTSTOR:	Ahh – that was good but why are you putting our drink into the stream?
ANGLATOR:	You will not have to carry it. Let us go.
METAPHOR:	Your load is lightened but I carry on.
ANGLATOR:	Let us go.
SPORTSTOR:	I tire again.
ANGLATOR:	The let us stop again, this time to eat and leave the extra food in a tree.
METAPHOR:	I'm beginning to see your method. Our load gets lighter as we go but on the way back we will have food and cold drink awaiting us without having to carry it.
ANGLATOR:	Yes, this is the type of new problem that must be confronted when we go to new places. See how much easier it can be to plan and have everything we need? Coming back down, we will only have fish to carry and I have brought the wicker creel with the comfortable strap for you, Anglator.
SPORTSTOR:	Oh, well, thanks for that consideration.
METAPHOR:	Yes, it was obvliously carryfull consideraction.

July 7

we went west seeking the THING
and, along the way
DOING and BEING
until we were stopped by water
without the right ship
we stopped
the new west,
altho i have never seen the difference
seems to be in places unpopulated
and the only 'new'
is what i or others bring to it
as it always was

i avoid the cities and only stay shortly in the towns
the west calls and the towns stare
what is a town but a stopping place for the journey
when the traveller said that the trip had been long enough
i carry on
some say that the earth is round
              (i can take their word for it)
and that the traveller will eventually
       run out of new places to go
and end up back where he started
              (i can take their word for it)
but right now
i think the reason these towns and cities are where they are
is that travellers moved too fast and then stopped
i move slower and will probably have more to do
at least i know i want to see this for myself

July 8

i carry with me
those books i always intended to read
but couldn't because of the constraints of time

between fishing and necessity
i find time to read
and open a new book
a pencil is still the best bookmark
because it is there when i need to note
and someday i may want to refollow
the marked map
to see where i have been
or i may need to remember
something i forgot

i may never consult these texts again
but then again i may
for now, i instinctively note those ideas
that seem to be in order

time allows this contemplation
without pressure
for a while, anyway
and i revel in't
and at the words
of other travellers
who moved slowly enough
to see and write and leave
things
for me to find.

July 9

somewhere back there,
someone thought i should be found and told
that a friend had fallen along the way
i have no adequate response
whatever i would say can no longer be heard
i cannot get back in time and so stop for a moment
and consider the memory

i must go on, i think
in spite of the change
and altho i had not seen the friend in a while
it was comforting to accept the presence
as it is saddening to accept the absence

i know, altho abstractly
that i will someday fall
but not this day
it is an awareness that i carry
of my mortality and frailty
and so i wonder what to leave
as a remembrance for those who go on
and conclude that
the BEING and DOING
will have to suffice

i walk to the stream to light a candle
and set it on a rock
by morning it is gone.

July 10

it is a long way from the black hills to albuquerque
but the irony is that it gets less green the further travelled
the trade-off is that other colors, pastels and fluorescents,
come into the picture

intensity lessens as the lifestyles transform
but the bottom line is that this may not be
a right direction

and so,
i have to distinguish between a
        direction
and a
        perspective.

perhaps i will learn as i go
that is my plan
        what am i saying?
that is my life.

i don't think i run away from anything
as a seeker, i move toward –
the question i face now is
        whether what i seek is there waiting
or whether i look in the right direction
        with the right perspective

these thoughts disturb me sometimes
and i come to the realization that i am spending
        too much time travelling
and
        not enough time fishing

July 11

the fisherpoet stands
overlooking new waters
reading the currents for tricks
a new cast must be made
for addressing new problems
so he draws upon what he has learnt
and enters the river slowly
soon a trout is caught
a leaper and climber that tail-dances and flies
up close it contains the myriad colors of the sun
fired by the spark of life
and yet all trout have this
each in an individual pattern
and finally the difference became apparent
in the background of the fishing
whether birch or pine or mesquite

the fisherpoet releases the fish
and contemplates the variance of the flora
pulling it into a place in memory
where it stands like a tin soldier
among friends and times and places
known so well so long ago
but still alive in the recess of the concrete
in the ideal forever.

July 12

there is a center to experience and to memory – the difficulty arises not from finding a center but in somehow maintaining it. i have often vacillated in my approach to this situation, but i have never lost sight of the goal of my quest. doubt edifies me with its presence however it may discomfort me at the time. i hope that i never lose sight of the grail or of the belief that it is there somewhere for me to find in the center of BEING and DOING.

July 13

well . . .

what do you think?

fate?

or

        luck?

    is there a book somewhere with our actions determined
      from which we merely portray our parts
      as reading dialogue from a play?

or
    do we live in the midst of random happenings
        and wander
      until random forces collide with
      what we perceive as our purpose
      (or the lack thereof)?

in other words:

    did i catch a large trout
      because my existence required it
      or because i learned the skill in spite of my purpose
      or did it just happen because i was on the stream
      at the same time the trout felt
      a random pang of hunger?

i . . .

    do not choose to overstate my own case
    i cannot take credit for all yet
    i cannot believe that all is forewritten

i . . .

    choose a center path in which things are purposeful
        and worthwhile
    yet in which i must make choices to continue
    there would be no need for worry if all were
        predestined
    there would be no need for worry if all were random
    but, truely, there is no need fur worra, worra, worra,
        because

i do what i can – as well as i can – when i can – thusly

plusly –
>it is impossible to fish and worry at the same time
>so i have been told

July 14

do you doubt your senses –
>or your belief?

i have come to a consensus
in a manner that brings me a smile
i have belief in, among other things,
>my senses.

when i see a flower or smell its aroma
when i hear a quail call at sunset
>or taste the juice of honeysuckle

or when i hold a trout in the palm of my hand
>and savor the moment –

i see the design to life in the pattern of it
form is function, and the reverse
but all works together in symmetry
leading to perfect balance
and i find that i need not necessarily seek the center
but that i am there already
>if i just do not waver

from what i instinctively understand
it is all there apparent in the design
and the only way to avoid the understanding
is to purposefully move away from center

do you doubt not?
then how can your quest be purposeful
total acceptance leads to misunderstanding
>of the design

doubt freely in order to accept
for lack of discrimination may lead you
>away from the center

balance your doubt and embracing
as you balance all in life
and you can not avoid the center
good and bad
young and old
all have a center
sense and belief
will tell you that.

July 15

i have no answer for why some things happen
    i have seen things happen to good people
    for no apparent reason
    and yet
they profit from it
    this does not mean that these people needed these
        bad things
    but that they had a buried spark within
    which could not come out until tested to the utmost

yellowstone burned mightily but now is enriched
    by the clearing
    some pine cones only open for rebirth
    when heated beyond the degree of everyday life
    and only the rage of fire can open them to
        fulfill their purpose
how clever of nature to have placed a cone there to
    replenish the forest
    whether cleared by man-made fire or
        lighting-caused devastation
how clever to have put the spark for overcoming within
those who are given a trial by fire so that it can emerge
    when times are right
there is always a balance to things,
    but that may not be apparent until a trial occurs
    and the scales of justice prove to be natural
        rather than man-made

but i have seen – nay, have lived this:
> for every bad thing that has happened to me
> a good thing has happened
> in proportion to the pain
> i have had joy

the hardest part is remembering this during the trials of life
> the hardest part is believing this
> > when the evidence is so against it for a moment
> > but it is there.

July 16

the camper was close quarters but that did not matter one whit because neither the setter nor i could get around well; i nursed a back injury sustained by overapplication of work but the setter had panicked when cherry bombs had been set off next to the camper and dived through a camper window to land on a highway in the path of an oncoming truck, after which he crawled into the woods to assess his injuries and i crawled through the woods looking for him and it took twenty-four hours to find him but i did and took him to a kindly vet who said not to worry that he was badly injured but would pull through so i waited in that town until he could travel and fished a small pond, catching bluegills and bass, and finally got him from the vet and we went on down the road to another town to rest and give our bodies time to heal but it was a slow process and we sometimes did not feel like getting up for a walk even though there are necessities in life which must be addressed, so we did get up when we had to and the setter and i would walk for a distance (we found we could go about one eighth of a mile in an hour if we tried) in spite of the pains and then withdraw to the camper to sleep, rest, and read and heal but one night, after a long hot day, we both felt restive but tired and each of us made our own funny sounds as we fidgeted with the sounds of crickets in the background until finally the setter moved slowly to the door and started scratching while i in my underwear attempted to get up to open the door for him and though i wondered whether i should put a leash on him i did not, thinking that he would just go right outside and come right back in and when he suddenly leapt up with a small cry and started running i worried and thought i should bring him back before he got further injuries and even though his running appeared to be in slow motion, mine was too, and if it weren't for the lateness of the hour i would have gotten dressed but i did not, thinking that i could surely outrun him quickly but i was wrong and we went down the lane for several hundred yards and passed a parked but empty car, or so i thought until the heads raised from the seats and the eyebrows raised on the faces and i wondered what they thought so i put on all the speed i could muster and caught the setter and walked, as normally as i could, leading him back toward the camper where we resumed our routine of resting, sleeping, reading, and healing, but with a new reality: we both knew we were going to survive this ordeal.

July 17

i sometimes fish for bluegills
they are a worthy quarry
willing to rise to a dry fly and to enact an epic struggle
they are a prolific and yet special fish

sometimes they bring me back to youthful days
of canepole technology and barefoot treks
to ponds and creeks abounding with life –
tadpoles, crawdads, frogs, shiners, snakes, turtles,
birds, raccoons, muskrats, dragonflies, deer, possums,
snails, flowers, trees, grasses, bushes, vines, mice,
mayflies, butterflies, ants, grasshoppers, ducks,
        and all the rest.

i cannot worry about trout when i fish for bluegill
altho i do feel a sense of gratitude to these little fish
for helping me to hone my fly rod skills

and now and then
restoring my humility when i erroneously accept the notion
that they are too simple to catch

tho i love trout and their world
i love the bluegill similarly
and have really enjoyed a longer affair
with these little fish
my gratitude is o'erbounding.

July 18

we floated the north fork of the white
seeking the trophy of remembrance
not the memory of triumph
e'en tho this is trophy water
which is to say
– full of trophs –
this, this veritable *autobahn* of canoeing
is, strangely, a source of wonderful fishing
perhaps embodying one of the
        myriadest experiences in its state
i fished the warm water section for
        smallmouth bass
        and goggle-eye
when the springs entered
        i drank from the water
        literally.
        i said, "literally."
        that is: LITERALLY!

then i caught trout
        browns
        rainbows

and all within gunwale to gunwale canoers
        shouting
        splashing

        bumping
but somehow not disrupting the feeding cycle
        of these inimitable fish

how can this be, you ask.
        balance.

July 19

i was once told
        that i do not do things
                the right way
which is one of the choices

i was further told
        that i do not do things
                the wrong way
which is, after all, another choice

but then i was told
        that i do not do things
                the navy way
a way that exists for things that must be

finally i was told
        that i do things
                my way
which seems to be mostly different

this struck me as rather humorous
        because
                i never made a conscious choice
to be different in the DOING of BEING

i just did things
        the way they needed to be done
                as they dictated
at the time i did them

i was always more interested
        in the DOING
                than in the *how*
and the BEING was just what it was

fly fishing is not a *how*
        it is a . . .
                form
allowing my own approach

the pome is not concerned with
        anything other than
                what i do
and the *how* is after the fact.

July 20

every now and then
i go back to the well
like a spring,
it draws water from inside the earth
and brings it to the surface

it is richer than purified water
containing minerals rather than chemicals
and it is filtered by the earth itself
rather than by mechanics

yet i find that some do not appreciate it
that they find it somehow lacking
they too go to the well
but for other purposes

these well-wishers have good intent
but miss the purpose
their energy is spent
upon things not the THING

how much better it is
to make something happen
than to watch it happen
or to wonder what happened
or to wish for something
that will never happen

July 21

the line lies in a curve on the still waters
drifting but slowly with the wind
and the nymph responds ever so gently
to the twitch of the hand
the lure is taken and the strike ensues
and the world is changed ever so slightly
but for the better

is a drop significant to the ocean?
it is in the sense that billions of drops
are what form it
but is one drop a matter for concern?
how can it not be?

does not this one suspended moment
affect all that follow
and does not this one experience direct
my actions toward or away from others?

i catch this trout in exclusion of others
whose choice determines that?
well, mine perhaps
or the trout's
or perhaps our mutual acceptance
of the terms of the contract

the result of this agreement is that
we each pass through the moment
and emerge with gained wisdom
neither of us could discern the outcome

in the process
even tho either could have influenced the moment

so this one moment came together
and the experience occurred
and each moment is similarly loaded
with potential for perpetual change
if we do not abort it.

July 22

ANGLATOR: What, if anything, do we get from this constant meditation? Do we find answers or attitudes? Are we enriched by the questioning or would we be better off to just accept? I know my own thoughts in this regard, but I want to hear yours.

SPORTSTOR: Is this a test? If so, I am not prepared. I have been trying to sort all of this but it is too much sometimes. I find I have a great store of questions and problems but I have no conclusions. Why do you do this to us now?

METAPHOR: Ha! You missed the point. He doesn't test but rather offers. There are no answers to that question other than what you yourself feel serves as question.

SPORTSTOR: Is this true?

ANGLATOR: Metaphor, sometimes you amaze me. I have often wondered if you would ever be able to just state things the way they are. And yet, I still have no evidence that you grasp my meaning in the way you have divined my intent.

METAPHOR: A warped bird seldom flies at night.

SPORTSTOR: Eh?

ANGLATOR: Perhaps I should reconsider.

METAPHOR: My meaning lies not in the words chosen

	but in what I charge them with. Your meaning may be something entirely different, but that is as it should be. I can have my meaning and you can have yours. Does your sky have a measurable limit?
ANGLATOR:	Well, what do you know about that?
SPORTSTOR:	I know that I am glad that it is his turn to carry things for a while.
ANGLATOR:	Very good.

July 23

i pull a book from my pack
and ope to the dog-eared page
the words recharge me
as they have oft

the weight of the book in my pack
is offset by the lightness added to my step
how many burdens can claim this?
i read hungrily.

devouring the ideas
i rest by the path
replenished, i move on
seeking what will be there

often i have trod this path
but never can it be taken for granted
that i have seen it all
despite the familiarity

never can i assume that any other
has travelled this selfsame path
or seen what i have read
e'en tho it appears so obvious

fecundity
ambiguity
propensity
aspiration

July 24

i am transformed
from under the surface
i wait and watch
for victuals to drift by
in my lie i am secure
and defend it from others
who only trespass by virtue of size
heading upstream,
i face the drift
and struggle to maintain
my position in the flow
dissipated by an enormous boulder
while i feed upon the nymphs and terrestrials
i follow my pattern
disdaining the odd
altho i observe the particular
it is only when i let carelessness intrude
or succumb to greed or laziness
that i feel the sting of the hook
and the relentless pressure
pulling me from the security
of my chosen lie
ignoring the shadows
i head for the depths
yet find the pull undiminishing
and so reverse myself
soaring through the sky
but still cannot free myself
i tire
and tho not giving up
cannot prevent the pull from directing me
the shock of the grasp i am in

is prelude to my surrender
but then
the stinging pressure is gone
and i am free again
pausing for breath and equilibrium
i remove to the security of the lie
with caution i resume my purpose
having new knowledge of pitfalls
having new awareness of the illusion of appearance.

July 25

i camp high on the mountain
alone? of course not.
alone is a construct of man
defining a concept that cannot occur
in nature
as *perfect vacuum* or
absolute zero or
any other conceived idea
(plato to the contrary,
ideas and things may sometimes be different
because imagination precedes reality)
i have never been alone
unless i mistakenly thought so
who or what is with me?
whatever or whoever i am has brought
everything i have ever done or seen to this place
and every moment increases my wealth of companions
i camp high on the mountain
revelling in the abounding comradery
the thing is:
i could never find myself *alone*
unless in a *perfect vacuum*
at *absolute zero*

July 26

do you think me selfish?
think what you will.
your perceptions cannot alter what is
but i will tell you this:
i am an american,
a midwesterner at that –
and i value my independence
as opposed to my individuality.
i understand that you could perceive
individualism as selfishness
it does involve putting self first
but i speak of independence
and respect yours
as i expect mine to be respected

do you see that this empowers you
to do what you may?
i neither ask for nor offer assistance
but i will help you if you need it.

take this for what it is worth.

July 27

sometimes i can think of nothing more knoble
than righting a pome
it may be more important than reeding one
language has pauwer
and the yuse of it
gives meening
i dont take creddit
for creeyating anything
but rather in terpretting
ideeyas
so shood i follow
the ruwells

if no one other than mice-elf
is goewing to reed this?
sumtymes i feeyul a
"responsibility"
to the reeder
and trie to emploi form
whooze choyse izzit ennyhwae?
yurz oar myne?
i merely offer this
it is up to you what to do with it.
ferrynuff?

July 28

In an old dead tree
An owl hoots and stands his perch,
Wearing night goggles.

Books,
Old, New –
Informing, Entertaining, Educating;
Keeping yesterday for today,
Knowledge.

Out by the well house
A raccoon hunts for supper,
In his bandit mask.

Coffee.
Warm, rich
Soothing, waking, maintaining;
First thing every morning.
Fuel.

Down by the spring branch
A deer sips the cold water,
As he wears silence.

Jeep.
Rusty, trusty.
Driving, climbing, pulling;
Always gets me back.
"Homer."

Across the meadow
Irish setter runs and leaps
In a cape of red.

Trout.
Lively, beautiful –
Leaping, swimming, feeding.
The flow of life.
Rainbow.

From the clear water
The trout leaps into the air,
Dressed in a rainbow.

Doing . . .
Savoir faire
Being, seeing, relating;
"Knowing how to do."
Life.

In the lofty sky
An eagle rides the updraft,
Wearing a headdress.

Cabin.
Cluttered, comfortable
Sheltering, containing, protecting;
"There's no place like
Home."

July 29

it is raining
but i cannot stay inside
nor will the red setter
ponchos were created for days like this
and so i drive the windy road to the platte
the hike from the jeep is long and the path slippery,
but i have my hikers on and my gear in my pack
soon we reach that place in the stream
where big boulders deflect the current
waterspots on the river obscure rises
and so i tie on a nymph.
drifting the brown fly under the jutting rocks proves
        productive
yet i wish for a larger fish today
and so i climb the bluff overlooking the river
on the edge, i wonder at things:
that people feel compelled to jump lemming-like from heights
i feel the instinct to avoid the slippery edge
but as i look down
i see the forms of trout in the current
and move closer
picking my quarry, i move back to the river and fish
long and long i fish
finally catching the big brown
looking up i see the setter on the bluff

July 30

i revel in my freedom
whether it is self-created or inherited
the setter taught me this
and many other things
as i follow him down the trail
i wonder who directs our travel
i sometimes hold the illusion

that i am in charge and determine our travel
yet it is he who reminds me
when i should awaken
and when i should open the door for him
in the long run
we probably follow individual paths
leading to concurrent destinations
neither of us leading or following
but sharing a journey
as comrades
learning from each other
without dictating
truly the essence
of freedom.

July 31

as i traverse the last hill
i discover the ocean
i am after all an explorer
tho not a famous one
is my accomplishment any the less
simply because i did not find it first?

with that in mind
did columbus really discover anything
i find it hard to believe that he
"discovered" a continent
that had been inhabited for centuries

i hold to the belief that
he discovered it for himself
as i did the ocean
perhaps i should note the day
and celebrate it every year

i have discovered other things
and written them down

as much for myself as anyone
but they are more true to me
having found them for myself

should i write them down
and celebrate them
as we observed the dates
of great discoveries?

i do.

August

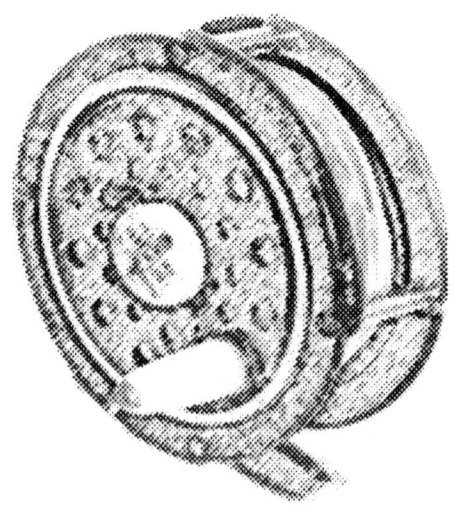

August 1

Days of dogs
Days of fire
Days of fireflies and fairs

Every dog has his day
and this might or might not be mine

the heat surpasses belief
and the dust swirls in miniature tornadoes
what's my beef
it's heat and mosquitoes

and the only place to go
where time is suspended
and where the whether
is bareable

is to a spring branch

where trout slurp hoppers and ants
and a terrestrial floating
without drag
may bring respite

from the heat

August 2

Having a good altitude helps

it seems as though the higher one gets
that is – the closer to the sun
the less the heat offends
and it is easier to breathe
despite the thinner air

and sometimes
around sunset
life emerges in full force
and trout not apparent in the shallows
remove from the depths of pools
or under logs or boulders

and crickets and frogs
take over the shift
from deerflies and bees
and a hatch will be on

but matching the hatch is more crucial
because low water makes cautious troutfellows
and there is no more snowmelt
except from the eternal glaciers

but whatever there is feels good
altho there is not much to share

August 3

Sometimes a river
like lifeblood
becomes the source
for exploration

By midwestern terms, this is no river;
    a river is big and muddy and slow
and the seeming veins flow into it
but by western terms this clearwater crick is a river
and the obsession for owning or controlling it has taken lifes
and blood has flowed in it

and the German browns swimming in it
who maybe came from Ireland
or Scotland
seem eternal

but were once just pilgrims
as I am now
looking for a place
of comfort
food
and safety

and I cannot help but think that they seem
       to belong to this place
as my Scotch-Irish-German ancestors did
running not from monarchies but toward democracy
bringing with them a fish embodying democracy
who will strike not the most expensive lure
but the most sagely presented

and who, like my ancestors
seem to wax poetic at inopportune times
and find fulfillment in BEING
and glorifying in whatever stage of the cycle
they may be in

in this
river

August 4

The true gold in the creek is not the soft metal
but the glorious reflection of the sun from the flanks
of browns rainbows brookies and cuts
populating the stream

following the waters to the source,
it is hard to imagine that this rapid creek
(by western standards; which, oddly enough
measure deer antlers by half as many points
       as an eastern count)
once carried away cars buildings homes and persons
until the source is reached

and the DAM juts into the horizon
once it broke and provided more water than manageable
to a city whose lifeblood depended upon it
and upon the very rocks of the mountain

and some reflected upon the power of nature
altho they seemed to forget that nature didn't put a dam there
and they seemed surprised that a man-built structure
could not withstand the pressure
and that all waters would seek the sea – eventually

but now
the creek is peaceful
and the dam has been rebuilt
and the turista swarm the villages
on motorcycles and in motorhomes
dragging motorboats
except in this creek

because it is too small to attract any
but those who KNOW
that small waters hold big secrets
and a fish measured in inches
looms larger than one from the reservoir
measured in pounds

August 5

it was harry who said to stay out of the kitchen
    you know
    that bit about standing the heat
harry told me
    never to trust a mechanical drag
(different harrys; same quality advice)

putting the two together –
    i go north to escape the heat

        and fish for big smallmouth
        and northern
        and walleye

my adjustable drag
        (cleaned and lubricated, of course)
is screwed down tightly for setting the hook
and when i hook a northern leviathan,
i reel when i can reel
and backreel when i must
but i stay out of the heat
and i never trust a mechanical drag

August 6

it is welcome cool in the main current of the river
especially as the sun begins to show
the radiating warmth buffets my head
but the cool of the water o'ercomes it

in midday, the trout will don lethargy
not from degree but from lack of oxygen
which the heat takes from the water
i will rest in shade and eat a lunch and read

some spots will offer protection to the trouts
and in them fish will feed
those i will shortly seek
after my own feeding

the book i hold is an old friend
and only sections need to be read
in order to relive the adventure
of the entire work

this stream is an unknown entity
new spots are surprises
and must be plumbed for understanding

must be cerebrally mapped for knowing
it might be that a new book would be better
but i wonder at the state of mind it would take
to sort a new river and a new book at once

would either be justly served – and would i?

August 7

across the mountains
to the desert
where the rivers all run to a different sea
i find streams flowing past colorful rock
without the familiarity of green surrounding
sunrise at these locales
offers the myriad of pastels
seen before in sunsets
presenting the illusion
that the sun rises from the mountains
yet i did not see it do that from there
do the rockies paint the sky?
or do colors spray from the peaks?
my time in colorfulrado did not prove or no.
i have been told that the colors
are just refraction of white light
which indicates heat
but i do not have to know this
to look
or remember

August 8

it is hot
the river is low and clear, yet
still cold in the depths
where trout hide
i waderless fish the pools
early and late

avoiding the noonday sun
a better time for sleep food or book
life breathes in the rising of the sun
holds the breath through midday
and releases it slowly at sunset
my clock ticks days rather than seconds
the pendulum moves so slowly
as to not evidence motion at all
i fish slowly
without the rush of springtime
but with no less intensity
a bend in the stream
where the stream bounces from a concave bluff
presents a large brookie
rare for this river
i release her
she pauses at my feet for an instant
and caudals across the riffle to the bluff
where she feels at home
and safe

August 9

terrestrials are appropriate
for low clear water
i fish hopper, ant, and beetle patterns
now and then
in lieu of my reliable adams
these offer an alternative to a trout
who has tired of common stream food
a terran insect is alien to the waters
easy pickin's for a quick-reflexed 'bow
but not often available
i was once a terrestrial
but now adopt amphibian attitude
which is probably the only thing
that enables me to survive
trout do not sip a beetle

as they do a delicate mayfly –
they take with a slurping relish
as though this unusual meal
requires different gustatory practice
few hoppers survive
in the realm of the brownies
bad luck for them
but good for the trout
and for me
as i tie a deerhair hopper to the leader
cast it to the head of the pool
and watch the brown devour it.

August 10

life is like a river
        (now there's an original thought)
wait – there's more
it flows smoothly to the sea
        (right)
and it branches and twists and falls and is deep
in some places
it can be shallow and fast
or slow and murky
        (how much more of this?)
it symbolizes . . .
        (yeah, yeah – i get it already)
look, is it that discomfiting for you
to hear it one more time?
have you learned this lesson completely
not just so you know the words
but what the words mean?
have you taken what you have learned
and applied it?
have you done anything yourself
with what you know
or do you just shroud your lack of action
in your cynicism?

(of course i do.
and who are you to question me?)
i'm who you will be
when you realize who you are.

August 11

ANGLATOR: Where are you?
SPORTSTOR: I don't know. It seems so familiar, yet I have never been here before.
ANGLATOR: Do you recognize anything?
SPORTSTOR: I don't know.
ANGLATOR: Tell me what you do see.
SPORTSTOR: We are on a river of clear water winding through a forest and occasionally coursing the edge of meadows. There are trees here whose form is similar to others I have seen, but the shapes are different. Trout are rising in the water, but I have to study the current to know why they are where they are. It seems we are on a place in the river that we have never been before. While it is like many other places on the river, yet it has its own character and is not like those familiar stretches we have fished before.
ANGLATOR: Tell me what you know.
SPORTSTOR: I know that, if I want to fish, I must read this new stretch and learn the common elements to apply what skills I have learned. Even though I have never seen this particular part of the river, still it has commonalities with other stretches.
ANGLATOR: Tell me what you do.
SPORTSTOR: I observe and I fish.
METAPHOR: So what do you fish, grasshopper?
SPORTSTOR: Terrestrials?
ANGLATOR: Very good.
METAPHOR: A "fair" assessment.

ANGLATOR: Well, you know what they say . . .
SPORTSTOR: What?
METAPHOR: What?
ANGLATOR: It takes one to know one.
SPORTSTOR: What?
METAPHOR: What.

August 12

it is too hot
to go to the well
and carry water

it is better
to wait
until the heat abates

the well is deep
the water cold
but cannot quench thirst

more must be found
a reason, perhaps
to seek so diligently

thirst sometimes seems enough
but need is stronger
and deeper

besides dipping the bucket
make a wish and count the seconds
till the pebble splashes

August 13

831 Rainbow Drive
Enihwair, MO 62550

Dear Sir or Madam:

    It has come to our attention that you have not responded to numerous queries that have been sent to your attention. It is then necessary for us to ascertain your whereabouts. If you do not reply in some way to this missive, then it must be assumed that you are not in the locale at the present time. Please take under consideration the ramifications of such a position at this time. We are going to have to change directions at some point, but without feedback from you, we will have to use our own discretion as to the direction and degree of change involved. This is not necessarily to be construed as a request on our part, but is merely a notification of impending alteration. We hope you fully understand at this point because further correspondence may be hampered by the lack of two-way communication. If you should find it possible to engage in meaningful action at any point, then please feel free to engage or elaborate upon the subject of our prior correspondence. In the meantime, we will not expect any response from you, nor will we even expect acknowledgement of this particular letter. We cannot assume that you got it or that you got any of the other queries, but we will continue to seek you out, to your advantage and to ours. Please feel yourself to be under no obligation to us in this matter, only to yourself.

Yours truly,

Lee Trachure
Questun, LTD

August 14

nobody told me about this
that i would be here alone
if they did
then i didnt hear them

the wind howls
but it is a hot wind, a *sirocco*
burning my flesh
withholding restoration

the sun will set
taking the dayheat with it
leaving a dry chill
necessitating a campfire

where is this place?
i feel uneasy here
and i do not know the direction
home

no one but myself
speaks here
i walk alone in the heat
hearing only the buzzing of flies

i think to sleep during the heat
and approach the water at night
when life comes forward
for a brief eternity.

August 15

the fisherpoet has a schedule to meet
following seasonal cycles
it is not like that of his cousin – the fisherking
who has an unhidden agenda

and yet it does correspond roughly
oddly enough, the wound comes to the fisherpoet
following the days of plenty
upon the realization of harvest
upon completion of the quest

the wound is invisible yet
its effects are pervasive
there is no champion for the fisherpoet
other than self
it is a lonely, yet fulfilling quest
ending in rebirth but
as birth – in pain
unlike the dominion of the fisherking
the fisherpoet holds stewardship
by choice and not by birth
foreknowledge of the wounding
does not deter him from the quest but
engenders it with no little poignancy
perhaps it is so with the trout king

August 16

it is an old green rocker in which i sit for hours and hours unable to move; pain wracks my back and prevents me from tying my own shoes. my most ambitious project is to get up and get a cup of coffee – it takes planning. i cannot go to the world for a while but the world comes to me in little ways. as i watch through the window, a canadian woodpecker lands on the sill and looks inward. i know what it is because the shelf by the fireplace holds books of birds and i can reach them. the bird should not be here – it is too early to migrate, yet there is no doubt that it is here now. perhaps it just felt a need to alter its proscribed cycle and see whether the southern lands are only green in winter. when it leaves i think of interruptions in my cycle other than this one now. once i smashed a knee in a fall, putting it through a case lid. once a window fell from a frame and imbedded itself in the palm of my hand. sometime later – although i didnt know it then – i would tear and rend the inner workings of a thigh in an incident involving a trailer and recently flooded land. as i sit there in the only comfortable chair i can find, the red setter lays his head upon my foot. he does not ask to go outside unless i happen to be up and by the door. he understands too well the situation – he is healing from his own wounding by a truck and many bones must knit. we both rest and heal. for a change, i reach for a book of native american lore and read a tale of the woman who meets warriors as they enter the afterlife. she is blind and feels the warrior for scars; if she finds scars, she eats them and allows the warrior to enter. if she does not, then the warrior must be blinded in the afterlife. i contemplate this and rest assured that both the red setter and i will be able to see in the afterlife – our woundings have been survivable but painful. the setter and i rest quietly knowing that the future holds other times for us.

August 17

i wondered at the riddle of the Sphinx
as i walked on three legs in the afternoon
sometimes four on the bad days
but i guess that the ancient stone thing
did not know me
or suspect that i would be different

but i was
and am
and probably
always will be

i walk slowly caning the path
the setter gimps next to the stream
soaking worn pads in the ripplicurrent
i would too, if i could get my boots off

the setter watches me like a tennis match
as i skip stones (no fishing today)
he watches me, then the stone, and again, and again.,
with no apparent desire to retrieve one

but we both know, or so he has taught me
that we will not give up
and that just being here today
is enough.

August 18

how odd that when i cast
i was only thinking of the line
when the lure touched down
a trout took it by surprise
mine and his, to be sure
but we had a deal
or at least I offered him one
if he would let me catch him
i would let him go
without even demanding
any further wishes –
as is common with golden fishes,
you know.
apparently, he accepted
because he did
and i did
and i did
and he did
and we both survived
knowing more
by just knowing that.

how odd that when i turned to go home
i smiled, wondering
whether or not that fish had truly meant
to wink at me

but he did
one wish is enough
when it is:
hope.

August 19

i once felt a confused spirit enter me
    not in doubt because of wrong choices
    but of inexperience and lack of choice
i wanted to help but could only offer what i had
    sufficient or no
it stayed with me – a part of me
    till it could no longer
    and sought my counsel
tho lacking the truth i offered sincerity
    and tried to ease its transition
    my doubts were founded
    and my desires for peace
so i offered the spirit sanctuary
    for what time it needed
    language fell short of communication
    all was through empathic translation
then the time came – the tunnel opened
    and vision came foggily
    i needed to direct
    but i knew so little myself
i indicated what i thought to be the path
    as best i could
    to bring the spirit to rest
    and it went on
the loss of this spirit diminished me
    but its travails required it go
    and insisted i facilitate this
how can i ever know
    if i did the right thing?

August 20

travel is best at night
especially when
the sun bears down
upon a jeep w/o AC
a breeze is created

the map is marked,
but only for so far
not for an intimate
but intermediate
destination

the blue line is
how we go
the red circle is
where
the green square is
layover
the black numbers are
mileage
the yellow marks are
days
the orange ones are
towns
the brown stains are
coffee
the purple ink indicates
friends

there was no way to know
any of this
until it was being done
after being dreamed
and recorded for
no particular reason
except to jog

an overworked memory
there is as much to forget
as there is to remember
sometimes.

August 21

at times,
i meet others in passage
we pause to compare experience
to share what can be told

we note what lures have brought success
or ones that have not
at these times it is possible
to discern the aficionado

all will ask:
how's the fishing
but the answer offered
carries portents of purpose

one may discuss size of fish
another may relate numbers
still another may decry the weather
or bemoan the "good old days"

but the true fisherpoet or his kin
will offer the only answer that he can
in light of his quest:
the fishing is fine.

August 22

i head into the mountains with the red setter
        we seek cool environs
snowcaps of spring are now gone
        but the thin cool air is refreshing

    melting glacierous caps provide icy knives
        that cut into heated feet
the overall effect, between fire and ice
    is balance

i park the jeep at the turnout
    we can follow the stream from the road
the hill descends into a valley
    and the river flows under a bridge
in the shaded waters
    i feel a chill
an odd feeling at this time of year
    when my shirt is sweat-colored

i wonder how long we must wait here
    before the heat storm passes
lightning forks between the peaks
    but no rain is in attendance
we pass the time in the valley
    letting the world pass over the bridge
while underneath it – time suspends
    offering respite – restoring will

August 23

so . . .
i explore the green
from its source to its fall into the high plains
when it crosses that desert, it moves fastly
trying to hold its store of oxygen and chill

the shallows insulate the main body of the river
carrying away the radiant heat
while the main channel sneaks by
belying its chill depths

then . . .
i wait till the sun falls

when the cooling volcanic rock releases its heat
when the shallows absorb the chill
and the trout move out to feed
only then, under the no-mooned stars
will i find the big browns feeding
as they search for smaller feeding fish
who, in turn, seek microscopic caddis or shrimp

what . . .
do the little fish think as they feed and flee
what do the browns think as they feed and avoid me

when i look over my shoulder,
am i keeping my cast out of the trees
        or checking for what stalks me?

August 24

i do believe in dreams
        too many come true
i do believe in many things
        too many to count

i had a dream once
        on the high plains
it hasn't come true yet
        but it may

i saw a deer, an eagle, and a bear
        locked in a struggle to survive
at times i was one
        at times another

i kept wondering –
        what is there to cause this?
they are not natural enemies in any way
        why would they struggle so?

i avoided the obvious interpretation
        and sought ambiguobviousity
because how things are
        can be paradoxical and true

all survived, in my dream, yet –
        none escaped unscathed
in time i accepted the dream's vision
        but i have never accepted fate.

August 25

what (if anything) is:
"fair"
?

is it when things are even and balanced
        equitable
        unbiased
or a time of comparing harvests
        of crops and herds
        complete with a carnival
or is it just average
        not superior
        but not bad either
        just middlin'
        tolerable
which wouldn't apply
        to a maiden
        or the weather

        ?

or is it misunderstood
and really:
"fare"
?

which could mean sustenance
>food for body and soul
or the price of a ticket
>for an easier journey
or an action letting another know
>how it is going
>well or badly –

would fare well equate with farewell
does farewell always mean fare well
>?

what does the fisherpoet mean
>when asked how it goes
and he says:
>"fair"
without spelling it
>?

August 26

i never saw the one that got me
or heard it or even suspected
what do you make of that?
i paid attention for all but an eyeblink
but that was enough.

someday i'll look back and smile
to think of all that happened
then i will know how and why
and accept it if it matters
and that will be enough

i did before and that's how i know
i can do it again
it doesn't take much to see the pattern form
once the wheel makes a full turn
and that's all it takes

cast to it; lead it; wade in it
take it to your heart
just always remember:
you will be the only one to ever know –
i just hope that this will be enough . . .

August 27

how goes it now?
well, i hope.
tell me your story as we sit by the fire
have another cup of coffee
it's still warm
do you travel far
or are you from around here?
do you know this stream
or are you learning it,
as i am?
share your story – there is time now
in the brief pause between sun-cycles
i would like to know
partly because i am curious
but more because you walk in my direction
have you seen the bluff pool?
you might like it
the current bends under the rock
and whirlpools whisk flies to feeding trout
have you fished it yet?
try it
what brings you here –
the fish or the fishing
the mountains or the river
the air or the fire
or do you know?
tell me your story –
now that you have heard mine.

August 28

so . . .
all the elements are always there but in different proportions
air is warmer now
water is warmer now
earth is warmer now

it looks to me like fire has taken over
        overshadowed, so to speak
heat produces light produces heat produces light
things are being done in the light of passion . . .
        the heat of reason

the spark is lost in the inferno
one hundred degrees in the shade
no breeze in sight
(but why look when feeling is what counts?)

get in the water
cast to the shade
go deep
take the time to . . .
appreciate what you see & feel
without hurry
it is time to enjoy things that are

so . . .
do not judge at a time like this
let the heat flow from you
        through you
                around you
                      in you
don't fight it
        there will come a day
        when you will need to
so . . .
        save your strength

August 29

ANGLATOR: It is time to turn around before it cannot be turned. When the line has run all the way out, there are only two choices: reel in or let it break. If you try to follow then you will be carried past where you can return from. You need to know when it is time to turn.

SPORTSTOR: What if there are better spots ahead – must I turn away?

ANGLATOR: It will be up to you to know when and where to stop, but do not stretch so far that the line breaks after you have followed. Either commit to pursuit or know the limit.

SPORTSTOR: And if I go past the limit?

ANGLATOR: Then you will not be able to return, but if you return at the proper time you will be able to plan to go further the next time and ultimately get to new places. Temperance is, as always, the key to advancement.

SPORTSTOR: I understand.

METAPHOR: I recognize no limits – when I reach the end I transform to meet the occasion and reevaluate my context. I can carry on using whatever I have around me. If I started there and ended up here, then this will be my start when I go elsewhere. Rather than stretching, I build upon what I gain until I decide to pass by the starting point again. I never turn back but keep going in a straight line that curves past its beginnings. A wave of light am I but still composed of particles. Time am I but still matter.

ANGLATOR: And so, to each his method, but still we sojourn together and coincide at points. It is important to know where we came from whether we know where we are going or not; the answer, of course, lies in that.

SPORTSTOR: Do we turn back together?
ANGLATOR: No. Even if we turn back at the same time and place.
METAPHOR: Onward to the beginning.
ANGLATOR: Yes.

August 30

so many years ago,
when the boy was born
in a northern city,
neither he nor his people
realized what lay in store
but none speculated.
where did it go?
was it enough?
should he have gone farther?
did he do good?
the questions came after he had embarked
and could not alter the direction.

he did not change the world
with white heat
but he did disappear.
changing the worlds of some
for the better
and for the worse
cold and empty
what would have happened
if he had been allowed more time?
and why
why
does the speculation only happen
now?

August 31

and what, when the fire is gone?
will life be different from this point on?
my lands, yes.
but it will continue
in non-pre-ordained fashion

ashes
but from them
the phoenix rises if it can
if not, then it will continue
in non-pre-ordained fashion

dust
cannot reveal the extent of life
it only indicates the absence
or former presence, anyway of a bust upon a shelf
no longer there

rain
washes it, not away,
but into the earth
where it becomes part of another cycle
contributing to the growth of lilies
and roses and oaks

shoots
rise from the earth
each fragile yet gaining strength
emerging from the darkness
into the painful necessary light

blossoms
indicate acceptance
of the terms of this life
and of the mortality
that is life.

September

September 1

already the trees project color
rivaling that of the most outlandish of trouts
not a time for mourning however
just another point on the circle
albeit without the anxiety and tension
concurrent with starting out

and the new growth has been replaced
with an air of maturity and preparation
for it is now that a season begins
not that another dies
and NOW is the time
and always has been

time spent on the spring branch
however
does gesture poignantly toward
the indicators that TIME
has set
and altho the harvest is in progress
it is not over

preparations are not yet to be made
but the moment is here to be doing
and i bask in the proof of the wealth
and i smile not at what has gone
but at what is

there is no ending but what
it is a beginning

September 2

i cast into new waters
seeking new mysteries
and the stream chortles over the rocks

at my clumsiness of effort
and at my outlandishness of attire

but i overcome my selfconsciousness
at being the new among the eternal
and let myself ease into the current
trying not to slip on the moss
or stumble over the stones

and i begin to see
as the sun peers through the alders
that nothing has changed as such
only the appearance is migrant
probably due to some shifting
of the earth and a different angle
of the lighted skybeams
refracting and disguising
all that i perceive with only one sense

but as i open myself to the waters
a warmth overcomes the chill
and i let myself be
and find that it feels right
and so it must be
because there is no reason otherwise
except for reason

and if i can just get rationality
out of my mind
i will be able
i will be concurrent
i will be
and
just
do
now.

September 3

altho i have never fallen in the current
      i know my day will come
and not exactly looking forward to it
      i accept its inevitability
and hope to face it honorably
      as much as possible
considering the circumstances

Jesus, everyone has to fall someday
      and a damn fall in the garden
is no better or worse way
      but different
once the realization that
      one has started to slip
and cannot do anything to stop it

happens.

and one of the only things
      possibly worse
is to knot know that it will happen
      or not be-lieve it
and to continue onward upward outward
      under that de-lusion
to the end

and so deciding that the best of all possibilities
      is rather to fall in the current
at least finishing
      doing what i do
i feel that my collar is too tight
      and loosen it and my tie
it binds me.

September 4

it is time now to go back to school
and that is where education really takes place
ofttimes in the going back
rather than in the school

mortality becomes apparent
and signs of it pop up
along the path
embodied in shapes

"Danger"
"Curve Ahead"
"Steep Grade"
"Stop"
"Yield"
"No Parking"
"No Passing"
"One Way"

responsibility impinges
and a sense thereof
gives a poignant flavor
to excursions of this season

like a melting memory of
a flavor of ice cream
that can no longer be found
like
      lemon freeze
different in taste
            texture
                      lingering flavor
                                and in satisfaction received
because the maker passed away
and didn't write down
how to do it

how to make it
he didn't leave a recipe at all
so now
> what can you do?

September 5

i guess i could make new ones
and those who had never tasted before
or held preconceived notions
of how it should be

would perhaps like this
and make new memories
because as it happens
one cannot live in the past

even

if one wants to

so

the idea is to remember snippets of the old thing
and try to incorporate them into the new thing
without letting on
that the new thing is not entirely original

i mean
that seems fair
its not like
i would be the first
to do something
like this
meaning
redefining

i just wonder
if it would be good
for those who
have an objective view
on down the line
let's hope

September 6

i woke up today
without any particular answers
i had no particular questions
no particular place to go
to do
to be
i didnt know what to think
the cocksureness of youth had fled
i had no clue

all, i guess, as it should be – somehow
the price of experience is stretching foundation
to the point where it becomes thin
the price of knowledge is lack of myopic surety
the price for letting go of misguiding principles
is the inability to march forward in a straight line

i cannot just sit and let this be
there is more – i know it
but the awareness that so much is futile
inhibits my actions
how ironic to spend time in not doing
while knowing how little time there is

perhaps i will remember, somehow
why and how i must do
i can remember the clarity
– at least in essence –
and i will find that and pay the price

for – what else is there to do?

September 7

it is too windy to fish, but
there are always dishes to be done
closets to be cleaned
the simplification of life to duty
eliminates the cloudiness of choice
i wash, rinse, and stack the dishes
and head for the attic
might as well
some stuff can be thrown away
to make room for other
or at least to make it easier to find
those things that are meaningful
three old footlockers summon me
the first contains nothing but the effluvia of
        prior memories
they mean little to me now, but remain intact
the second contains decorations from
        past events
these have gone by now, but will be kept
the third, however, contains paper and ink
        renditions of life experiences
i seek and sort looking for a clue
        old fishing licenses
        letters to and from
        school work
        cards
        pictures
        birth announcements
        death announcements
        warranties
        receipts
        marked calendars
        newspaper clippings

generations of stuff
it is in there somewhere
but what is it?

September 8

.When my father died
things were stored
and much later
i had to sort them
and i found an oldfolded piece of paper
that revealed

        Shaffer Engineering and Machining
              12 East Oak Parkway
                Detroit, Michigan

and when i turned it over i saw
a letter my father had written
when he was seven years old
written in a childish scrawl
and with the effect that gravity has
when writing on unlined paper

Dear Uncle Kady,
       How are you? I am fine. I am
looking forward to your visit. Christmas
is not far away. I am enjoying school.
              Love,
                     Tommy

Tommy was
first Thomas middle Kincaid
for Kady
first Thomas last Kincaid
and my son is
first Alexander middle Kincaid

and i could not help but notice
how like my father's hand was my son's
a few years back
and i could not help but think
that my son now
is older
than my father was then

and yet this letter is still here
though sender and receiver are not

September 9

did lancelot think himself immune
        from those things which plague the rest of us?

he found out differently
        his noble fall placed him in the realm of humanity
which was, in the end, as it should be

– aspiration, inspiration, perspiration, desperation –

not the seven deadlies but possible directions
avoidance is not necessarily proof of virtue
resistance is stronger but still lacking
true virtue comes from recognition of fault
and in the continuance of effort
in the face of awareness of human frailty

what ho, lancelot?

September 10

in the mountains, i see the clouds
moving and bumping, they ionize

the sky grays and dims
i can choose the road through the storm

or cut around the mountain
it will stop the storm

lightning already furies in the stratosphere
and the breeze uplifts and brings the scent of rain
altho i camp across from the lightning bowl
still i pack camp and prepare
i once saw a hundred year old oak explode
when a lightning bolt rammed it dead-center

then it starts
the first drops make individual sounds
that soon crescendo to a roar
interrupted only by thundercrashes
we sit in the jeep, feeling protected
knowing that such a fury will soon be spent

leaves and limbs and debris fall
footprints wash away
old gullies fill and new ones form
the water washes away all
the setter lays in the back seat
lifting his head when lightning cracks

after –
birds look to the damage in the trees
i muddy my boots exploring the earth
altho the storm still rages somewhere past us
the calm is upon us now
we walk

the air, like the earth,
has been cleaned and cooled
lightning has removed deadwood
is it any wonder that a primitive soul
– one who had suffered through a storm –
believed it designed by an omnipotent hand?

September 11

there is something vastly different
about fishing after a rain
the air is clear and cool
and the trout seem refreshed
a multitude of opportunity
has washed into the stream
and they feed confidently
as i fish

sometimes i fish to not think
sometimes to do that very thing
i never know the purpose
until i am in the middle of doing it
but whatever it is, it turns out to be
– appropriate –
i fish alone now
most have gone to other things
now that the carefree easy spring fishing
has come and gone

some have given up
no longer fishing the streams
some may not; some can not –
for whatever reason, they do not
i carry on, the best i can
just me and the setter

the tinge of red that touches the leaves
serves to remind me that i will one day stop
the poignancy of the moment is not lost
i become aware
so i watch listen smell taste touch all i can
because there will be a day when it is gone

September 12

the sun rose in the east today.
it was no surprise, but it was a reminder
i too came from the east and rose
i fell in the west
my cycle is lateral not arching, however
so i know it is time to pack and go home
the setter lays his head upon my knee
knowing our purpose he affirms
so we pack and take a final walk in the mountains
seeking a last vision to carry back with us
it is there in the utter lack of dramatism
in the knowledge that eternity lives here
how simple and profound it is
how direct and touching
this walk along the river relieves
the feeling that anything was ever lost
or that anything ever would be

we get into the jeep and i drive straight through
on the road i see other travelers
trying to find their various directions
the cool night affords good driving
and occasionally i turn on the radio
and listen to golden oldies
songs i have sung
life i have lived
feelings i have shared
reminders of where i have been

September 13

sometimes i wonder
it is fate or luck or what?
what is it that i follow
as i do whatever it is that i do?
but it all seems to come out all right

it seems to make sense
even without following anyone else's path.
sometimes the purpose
of what i have done
only becomes apparent
after the fact
that is a blessing, i suppose
because sometimes i might not
       have continued
had i known the reason
only in the overview
do i find total clarity

perhaps it is instinct
or a guardian angel
that saves me from some things
and tests me on others
or maybe i will never know
and just find myself there
without a clue
but, meanwhile –
i will carry on
as best i can
and try to do
whatever it is
that i do
the best i can
and try to do nothing
that harms another
and try to always
have hope.

September 14

will your philosophy get you thru rough times
or does it just rationalize "things"?
what do you do with your problems
if they overshadow your life?

you could think
you could drink
you could whistle
you could go fishing

it's up to you, you know;
whatever, just seek firm ground

some thought i ran away
'cos i went fishing to sort it out
they could not understand
that i could not fish and worry
at the same time, so . . .
i could look at "things"
objectively

September 15

but after that . . . i seek
       home
       balance
       familiarity
       comfort
       safety
       solitude

i drive all night
so that i can wake up
       in my own cabin
by the branch

i sleep straight through
after unloading the jeep
because it must be done
and then i stumble from the bed
make coffee
step outside
to straighten things out

i hear the echo of a meadowlark from over the hill
and breathe . . .
just breathe.

and unpack the tackle

September 16

it has been a good day. the red setter and i rest after wandering along the spring branch. the walking and looking and fishing have been good and we feel the weariness that comes welcomely from exertion. i pause in the brown chair and sip french coffee while my feet recuperate from the rocky path. almost dozing, i lean back and breathe in the memory of the day and attempt to store the detail so that it will always be with me, if not in words, then in context. the setter moves from his place at the mantle slowly. he finds that place welcome in the winter when fire warms the brick and in summer when the coolness is retained in front of the unlit fire. before i doze, his head rests upon my hand as a sign of comradeship and sharing. i scratch his head and ears, pausing on his wisdom lump and wondering of his method of storing adventure. i doze this way for a while and awake to find him dreaming at the fireplace. i wonder if he dreams in color, as i do at times like this. probably he dreams in scents and feelings, as i wish i could. both of us are necessary in perspective. i remember the fishing and the sights and sounds and he remembers the place. when he awakes, he brings a towel to tug-o-war and we do, after which i put a snack on his nose that he will balance there until i tell him it is ok. then he flips it and catches it from the air. we both take pride in this little trick because i taught him when he was ten years old, and too old to learn new tricks. i also know that he only does this because he wants to and apparently enjoys it equally. it took us long to learn to understand one another, but we do. as i fix our supper i reflect that these things he has shown me today may be the greatest to which i can aspire.

September 17

so, OF ALL THINGS
(which, by the by,
was my grandmother's
favorite interjection)
. . .
(mine, too
when i stop
to think about it)

i go fishing
(another of my
favorite interjections)

and head back to,
of all places,
where i began
(at least in
one particular cycle)

and find myself
(of all people)
back
at the spring branch

September 18

hello, old friend
it is good to share your waters
the familiar yet altered
flow of your new yet eternal current
is refreshing and comforting

once you loomed so large
but seemed to diminish
and one turn of my cycle
but now . . .

you show larger than ever
in your mental projections to me
and i glorify in your memory
and am thankful for your continued presence

oh, happy day
the prodigious son returneth
worn but wiser
or at least thinking so
at this point

i enter, i cast
and you appropriately reward my efforts
in your own time
in your own way

you sacrifice a trout to me
and i feel a rush of humility
wondering if i am worthy
or may be you are modeling
that type of behavior for me
so that i will not only understand
but will empathize
and ACT according

it is glorious

September 19

ANGLATOR: And so begins the lesson for today – take your tackle and follow me.
SPORTSTOR: What begins? What do you mean? Where are we going?
ANGLATOR: We go away from the stream – toward another search that will lead us to our answers. We will not fish, but we will carry the tackle because that is who we are. Do not question so. We will find an answer and

	the trek will be well worth it.
SPORTSTOR:	Of course I will, but it is most mysterious. How can this help in our fishing?
ANGLATOR:	You will see.
SPORTSTOR:	Why does that worker look with such disdain upon us? We have done nothing to bother him. And yet that one smiles, even though carrying a heavier load down the road. That woman scowls, but the child laughs. That man shakes his head while he drinks ale in the morning. That man waves as he digs in his garden. Why do they seem to perceive us with such differing vision?
ANGLATOR:	Perhaps they don't see us as who they are – but as who they are not.
SPORTSTOR:	Well, what does that mean? And why must we do this rather than fish?
ANGLATOR:	As I said, do not question so. The answers will come to you.
METAPHOR:	This dog has been following us.
ANGLATOR:	I hoped he would. This red setter belongs to a poet who lives in a cabin on the river. I have brought food to share with him and he will share his company with us. His ancestors lived by this river and he has many pups that will follow him. Pay him attention.
METAPHOR:	This is most strange; you are juxtaposing imagery that is paradoxical in nature and yet expect us to follow.
ANGLATOR:	As always, you have an amazing grasp of the obvious.
SPORTSTOR:	You know, yesterday when I walked past here, none of these people noticed me at all, other than to wave in passing. Today, when I carry fishing gear, they all have such amazing reactions. Have they not learned to sort their difficulties by removing

ANGLATOR: themselves?
There you have it. Here – take some food for the dog and he will allow you to give it to him.
METAPHOR: Is there a point to the setter?
ANGLATOR: I certainly hope so . . . else there is no point to me.

September 20

what a beautiful fall day
how the color edges into the leaves
i walk the stream i have found here
it is new but somehow familiar
the depths are mysterious
and i will have to sort them
rocks and logjams indicate current
watercolor indicates depth
i cast a nymph of squirrel hair
weighted to sink fast
it imitates a shrimp
but is impressionistic
rather than imitative
i wonder if it speaks to the trout
as it speaks to me
when i feel a tightening of line
i strike
and a fish is on
i give line as the trout heads first upstream
then into the depths
and turns for a run downstream
i move into the current
to head the trout back upstream
and it obliges
when finally i land the fish
it looks at me
as tho i were from another planet
i release it after admiring the color

and move on.

September 21

there is honor in bottoming out
tho it is not apparent to some
but it is the point that must be reached
to turn things around, so to speak
and everyplace is up from there
the trick is to not give up
it is to lock onto a glimmer of a spark
of a thread of a whisper of a hint
that something there is worth it
but if it is not easily obtainable
some look elsewhere
and fail to learn the simple thing
and are doomed to a cycle of error
repeating wrongs based on wrong choices
but the true irony of the whole thing is that
even tho i know this in my bones
and i understand why i feel this way
i pack and go again
looking for . . .

September 22

a place to fish
a beautiful, lucky, energizing, illuminating
        environ
i cannot go past water
        whether creek or stream
        river or pond
        lake or impoundment
        ocean or swamp
without wondering what is going on
        beneath the surface
is there room in that cycle for me?
do i belong at that spot
        rather than at some other place

when my father taught me to fish
    he had that answer
if there was a place to park the car
    then we stopped and fished
we took some long purposeful trips
    to rumored hotspots
but often we drove and found a new spot
    totally by chance
he would say,
    "it looks good"
and invariably be right
we found places overlooked by those driving by
    how did he know to do this?

September 23

there was a time
i left all my tackle on a shelf
as i did my books
i tried to do what was expected of me
and not fritter away my time
i worked ceaselessly and tirelessly
to provide the accoutrements
of
    the good life

and did the best i could
i told myself
that there would always be time later
and that i was doing something meaningful
i continued further down that path
accepting the false praise spewed my way
until i was brought to a screeching halt
    by fate
and had to sit in a chair
contemplating what next to do
    and why
    and how

i dont know what struck me harder
it could have been the futility
or the irony
possibly it was the emptiness
perhaps the falseness of measure
looking back,
i think it was just the lack of balance
maybe i emulated my washing machine
when it told me that it was time to stop
        and readjust
it had an out-of-balance alarm
        as, perhaps, i did
without realizing it.

September 24

i have learned
        (even as an old dog)
a new trick:
sometimes, what i think i should be doing
        is not at all what i really should do
if there is one thing that i have figured out
        tediously and painfully
that is it

the THING is to know when to change
what to DO is the question
NOW is the time
WHERE may reveal itself

i must leave myself open to
        change
        ideas
        beliefs
        purpose

in short,
        life

and not jump on any false bandwagons
no matter how appealing at the time

do you ever suffer doubt?
it is part of that list above
it is what strengthens all the others
it is the necessary component
i absorb doubt when i sense its presence
regarding it as a dear friend
as i regard you
if you accept me –
        accept my doubt
perhaps you will find the balance worthwhile

September 25

the red setter is ever curious
everything must be sniffed and prodded
it must be tasted and looked at sideways
fields must be run
water must be walked into
hills must be climbed
boulders must be leapt
and when all this is done
it is time to lie down
and dream about it

what a wonderful philosophy
he did not get it from any of my books
what voices does he hear
that guide him through his life?
he occasionally listens to me
but follows, rather, his own judgement
he must listen to the wind and the crickets
but surely there is more –
does he hear the seasons change?
can he smell the time of day?
do the stars spell out direction?

does he see clouds shaping plans?
do paths visible only to him
lead through the woods
        and across fields
        and through streams
        and over boulders?
i look at him puzzling over
        how he can know –
he returns my gaze, wondering
        how i can not.

September 26

i pulled a book from the shelf
        (it doesnt matter which one)
and read for a while
altho i had read it several times before,
it said new things to me –
answers were there to questions
i had not thought to ask before.
they were there just waiting
in case i ever needed them
        (and now i did)
the important thing is not
how long it took me to find them
but that they were there
        (both the books and the answers)
i wonder if and how i would have found
these answers if i had parted with these texts
as i once almost did –
actually,
i think it would not have mattered
once i knew what to ask
i think any book could have told me
that all are searching for an answer
holmes and christie
twain and poe
whitman and hemingway

and hamlet
all i had to do was put the book down
and seek
because it is all there
in the wind and words
in the streams and texts
in the water and rhymes
always was –
always will be.

September 27

Dear Sir:

    It has come to our attention recently that you have not been in attendance at our regular meetings. Since all our decisions are made by consensus, we feel that your absence has become a detriment to our efficiency. If you are attempting to exercise personal freedom or have become doubtful of the meaningfulness of our purpose, let us assure you that we sympathize with your plight, but we must carry on with our work.

    Unless we all agree on the direction of our organization, anarchistic ideas will interfere with our forward motion. Your input is valuable to us and must be presented so that we can eliminate any thinking that is counterproductive. As you surely know, things must be done the right way for everyone, and the best way to assure that this will happen is to make sure that we all do the same things at the same time. Please contact us to make arrangements for your readmittance to our organization before you find yourself "out on a limb," so to speak. We value your opinion and look forward to hearing it.

The Committee for Standardization of Purpose,
    in affiliation with The Right Way

September 28

i forgot to sort the mail today
after coming home from fishing
it was a good day
and i caught several fish
altho i dont remember how many
or what size they were
what i do remember
is that i watched a hawk soar
and a deer drinking from the stream
i saw a fox hunting in a culvert
and a raccoon catching crawdads
a red-wing blackbird observed me
        as it clung to a cattail
sculpins darted among the rocks
        in the stream
and a gentle breeze waved the cottonwoods
        setting seeds adrift
i reached into the stream
and found a petrified mussel
        which i kept
and picked up some trash
that a careless wanderer had dropped
        put it in my vest
i remember one cast that sought
        the edge of the reeds
and a trout that followed three times
        finally intercepting it
beyond these things
i have no words for the day
it showed me its *je ne sais quoi* –

September 29

the fluctuation of doubt
        may lead to assurance
or to more doubt – but i accept that

my own confusion is, no doubt,
simply misinterpretation of what is there
my sweeping thought
      does not always sort well
have you such incomprehension at times?
well,
i wont tell you what to do with it
im not sure i know, myself

i find myself confusing myself
i certainly dont suggest that i have answers
the only thing of which i am certain
is that i will keep seeking
and that i may or may not find answers
and that i may once again have belief
and that i may learn –
      something
to do or be or seek
it is not easy
at times i do not like it
clarity eludes me
purpose seems evasive
i wonder if the depths are
      where i should seek
or if that is my downfall
perhaps i should stick to the surface
reflective and distorted.

September 30

i walked in the garden today
a few, tho not many, things remain
gone is the green lushness, the fecund rainbow
i touch the earth
it is dry – no rain lately
the heat of august leached all moisture from the surface
no breeze to move the showerclouds into position
a good rain would energize the green

and put foodstuffs in the water for trout
bringing them out to feed
but there is no rain in sight
i walked by the stream today
it is low and clear
moving slower and adding less oxygen
trout conserve energy in midday
feeding early and late
i will fish tomorrow
but today, there is no relief in sight
the setter has found the cool
under the porch
it is there that he lays in a hollow
cut in the bare earth
somedays, i think to do the same –
find a safe spot and sleep there
not striving in futility
it is hard sometimes
to remember that there is balance to the cycle
that the cycle will swing up again
that something good happens for each bad
that tomorrow i may go fishing
even though today i wait
today there is no rain in sight
the fall is here

October

October 1

this is the point where we contemplate
        the american dream
                (as it pertains to the fisherpoet
        in particular –
                and people in general).
i (and many others) once assumed that
        the american dream
meant getting what was wanted
        whether rich free famous or president
but now i think differently
        i think i found it when i wasnt looking
it snuck up on me solidly
        and i took it
                (hook line and sinker)
so to speak.
you see –
        it is not:
getting what you want to get
or having what you want to have
or going where you want to go
or being president and presiding over
        this that or the other

what it is (simple though it may be)
is:
        BEing what i want to be
        DOing what i want to do
that's all folks . . .

now –
        who could ever stop me from this?
        who could say the dream died?
        who could say it was a myth?
        who could say that it was a product
                of a misogynistic ethnocentric
                        bunch of guys

                or that it was not real?
          the american experiment
(for such it was called)
       is ongoing
the data are not all in yet
so far – things look good
from my perspective

October 2

if i can be and do whatever i want
then i simply aspire to be
a good fisherpoet
not great famous rich or revered
        just: good
it is a full time job
the pay is not great
the hours are flexible
it is a way to see more and do more
without having to go too far
or do things out of desperation
simple yet complex
quiet yet musical
slow yet like lightning
peaceful yet epic
contemplative yet action-filled
confusing yet clarifying
straight and narrow yet broad and winding

more than just something to be
       it is something to do
it is not just a way of looking at life
       it is a way of life
so far, few have chosen this path
else the lines would be long
and so many would be waiting

quite simply,

it is what i want to be
when i grow up.

October 3

applicant: me
location: spring branch
education: sufficient
position applied for: fisherpoet
relevant experience: (see attached)
references: the red setter
         you
salary required: living
willing to relocate: why?

****

(attached)
some of my experience involved just a toe in the water
some, however, included total immersion
i qualify so you dont overcredit me in some areas
but here are some of the things i have done that relate:

             Fishing guide
        d Ishwasher
        mu Sician
       bucked Hay
    worked in a movi E theatre
       compute R person
         Photographer
        s Old guns
       luthi Er
      music Teacher

October 4

understanding comes in bits and pieces
acceptance happens gradually, but completely
knowing, at least, how and what to do

(thanks to rmk and maj)
i set my sights on it
(thanks to djw)
and persist
(thanks to aks, rls, tks)
there have been obstacles
(you know who you are)
and there have been wondrous friends
(you know who you are)
and so i can do this
and enjoy it
and learn by doing
do by being
accept what has been and will be
and what is
this is just a simple thought
and only took me years to find.

October 5

now i can fish with the long rod
free from the drag of silly things
i go to the spring branch
the red setter walks alongside
we do not have to speak
because we have come to accept
and understand, as best we can
our comradery adds to the day
and all experiences shared
as we walk along and in the stream

alders cottonwoods and scrub pine
line the bank with reds oranges and greens
huge oak leaves drift in the water
small hatches cloud the air
i tie on a number twenty adams
to match the little insecta
and cast to a smooth pocket in the current

a trout (neither large nor small) takes
and i play the fish gently
taking care to remove the hook easily
and cradling the fish in the water for a moment
before releasing it

then i spy the other trout
       (neither large nor small)
rising to insecta knocked from the branches
       of a downed tree
on the downstream side, it feeds with impunity
no cast fly can drift to it
i inch to within casting range
and lop the leader over a branch
and keep the line suspended
by lowering the line, the fly touches the water
the trout, fooled, takes it and i give line
until the leader is clear of the branch
and the line is on't
then a quick flip frees the line
and i play the trout
having jousted and matched.

October 6

the spring branch remains
       always
i have seen pictures of people on horseback
who came here before there were roads
it is an easier trek now, but no less appreciated
if there had been no road, i would have ridden
       or walked
to get here
and been glad of it

there are not many places like this
       yet
most places are like this

        because
it is not what is here
        but
what we bring to it that counts
        so
i choose this place
        even though
another might suffice
        and
i find it repays me
        and
demands only just endeavors

October 7

however –
i still have moments
wherein i come to grips with things
that must be
in spite of my efforts
not all things lead to complacent understanding
and sometimes things happen to pain me
and it is hard to retain that perspective

from the heights, i plumb the depths
and try to keep my head above the surface
and sometimes still have to wonder down the road
and wander why

sometimes it takes being past a thing
to see it
or to recognize the afterimage
burned into my optic nerve
by a flash of insight
into
paradise or pandemonium

October 8

It is time to break camp and move to another location
there is no barometer indicating that
                this camp is no longer good,
just a feeling that another location might be more conducive
to whatever needs now to be done

it is sad to pack the gear
and the red setter cocks his head
and bounds restlessly
he knows the motions of breaking camp
but does not feel the urgency

sleeping gear, cooking utensils, miscellaneous equipment
fits tightly into the panniers
like a puzzle

nothing productive is expected on this day

except movement

and a sense of loss

October 9

the top of the mountain is lonely
it is the place waters flow from
none remain unless frozen
in lower altitudes, i follow water to its source
here, i follow the water itself

angst dwells here
and why not?
this is the desert
the place from which all can be seen
but none touched

i could fall from here
but i could not survive it
others have proven this;
i do not need to experience for myself

why would a wise man seek the top
unless he was a false shaman
creating an illusion of alchemy
to make up for the inability to touch?

altho i cannot stay here
i have found my own vision here
and partake of leaving sadly
knowing that i will be saying goodbye
to a particular part of myself
one that perhaps i should have known better
for the good that it did bring me.

October 10

my cabin beckons me
and i find it
no other place is home to me
and no other place
is like it
i fish with new awareness
and find peace and discomfort
here and elsewhere
but accept the bad as leading to good
ultimately
i rig my gear for the spring branch
a different setup than i would use
on a large western river
or a high rocky beaverdam
and the point is no longer
      how many
      or how large
      or whether i catch fish at all

it is just to fish and partake of the experience
so . . .
      i go fishing.

October 11

now once the fisherpoet passes the need to catch
    the first one
    many in numbers
    large in size
and the particular fish stands out
then true appreciation enlivens each experience
and the catching can be significant
    altho not necessary

and i remember one particular day
    and one particular trout

after an unproductive day
    lacking in understanding

this will be one of those days
    but once it was not

this was
    first just another day
    then a special day
    then a day that mattered no more
        for its own reasons

the particular one that i caught
came to me coyly
ultimately took with gusto
swam the entire pool
seemingly aware of the tension
    of the line
i thought it caught but
it ran round a snag

past the swift depths
i could not disentangle it
nor could i release it
but it managed to entangle the leader
and in trying to free it
i broke it on my end
yet the other end remained fast
    to the snag
all i could do was watch
    from a distance
and wonder if it freed itself
    or wasted away

October 12

the fly settles to the surface
where it is taken by the trout
who leaps and dives and runs
circling the pool and cutting at angles
through the swift current
alternately launching skyward
then bulldogging in the depths

can you truly feel this?
no?
that is how it is –
this thing must be done
to be realized
and appreciated
if all it took was description
then vicarious visual representation
would suffice –
but it does not.

this thing must be felt
because that sense comes into play
it is why underwater films
of a wriggling trout fall short

and why films from the surface
showing a bent rod and a leader
disappearing into the depths
seem inadequate also

it is why water splashed on the lens
fails to moisten or cool
and why the current is unreadable
why the pines seem deodorized
and the camp cooking tasteless
no amount of second-hand imagery
can come close to
doing
the
thing
itself
so . . .

October 13

what is said here
may or may not make sense to you
depending on your
level of experience

just
seeing/hearing/tasting/smelling/touching
may not be enough
to make the thing alive for you
unless you have lived it
and then it can be a
     cue
to the clue
of the thing
and its reason
for being
or doing

i do the best i can
knowing this
and that i can not be there
beside you
to make sure you try
but i cannot just say:
    trust me . . .
that has always been the mark
    of distrust
i cannot say:
    i will not lie to you
for that could very well be one
    (not that i would intentionally)
all i can say is:
    this is what i have seen
    take it for what it is worth
    and i hope it speaks to you
    as it does to me
ok?

October 14

some look at fishing
    (or a pome)
only on the surface
seeing ritual virility
    or virtual reality
there is more
    much more
but only at certain spokes
    of the wheel
is this truly apparent
only at certain points
    of the cycle

the cast line falls in snake-like curves
straightening when a fish takes
    or when the current pulls it

opposites in character
> but similar in effect
and the difference is known
to the one doing the doing

October 15

so what now constitutes a lie?
you can make up your own definition, but
> there are characteristics.
there are words
> and there are meanings
try this:
> my last fishing trip
what does that mean to you?
> – to me?
it could be the final one that i make
or the most recent in a series.
it could be indicating a moment of sad epiphany
or a fond and recent recollection
so, you see –
> the words are not always the meaning
> or at least not all of the meaning
if i started out:
> "on my last fishing trip"
so now reconsider that earlier definition of
> a lie.
it surely means that you took my intention wrong
> if i intended it
words cannot lie; meanings – perhaps,
> but
intentions carry the responsibility
so ask yourself:
> who carries the intentions?

October 16

the jeep follows the turns in the mountain roads huggingly luckily. as i reach the pass the air chills and displays its meagerness of oxygen. this pass is just the first of many but already i feel the need to stop. finally there is a pulloff and i wheel the jeep in. a semi roars by rocking the jeep and me with the blast of the vacuum following it. as the chugging diesel rolls on down the mountain its dopplered sound trails it and soon stillness returns to the pulloff just after the pass. i look up and as my eyes adjust i see more stars than we ever had in the midwest and more twinkling colors in the cosmos. by being on a mountain am i that much closer to them or is it just the clear mountain air? as i ponder this a sort of vertigo takes hold and i reel having to grab the jeep for support. it is cold and hard to breathe and i am not sure which way is up for a moment. i orient myself on the hood and take a few breaths trying to suck some sustaining oxygen from the thin air but my chest hurts from the effort i think. maybe i should just sit and wait until the feeling passes. i open the passenger door and sit one foot in one foot out and look over the moonlit mountains. one after another as far as i can see. pines roughen the silhouetted edges of the peaks except for the very tops above treeline where rocks replace life. no signs of civilization are visible except for this road this jeep this me. the eternality of the mountains and the starry sky and the darkness of night converge at this point at this time. i finally resignedly take my place behind the wheel and begin my descent down this particular mountain. taking a breather helped and as the heater warms me i start to feel i've regained my bearings. i miss home and the fire and my books and the red setter. i think about them all in the midwest and myself here in the west. orientation comes back stronger and i glance at the north star. if it is there then this direction must be east. then somewhere over there must be home. and i must be generally homeward bound. at least i feel that i know which way is up.

October 17

meanwhile,
        back at the branch –
interesting happenings have been things
the waters still flow
the wind still blows
the trees still grow
the spirits still know
the natural foe
of whitman and poe
marches onward
        in time
yet is so unmitigatingly eternal
that i feel i stepped out of the progression
into a cycle
and, ultimately, back into the moment i left
even tho the stream has altered and cut
        its channel into new grooves
the essence of the waters is the same
        it is my essence changed
for the better, i hope
        but changed, nonetheless
i recognize the marks
        mark the twain
        mark the trail
        mark time
        mark, get set
        go
but return in time . . .

October 18

a myriad, a plethora, a multitude
        a cornucopia, a diversity –
a bunch
of attendant feelings accompany my cast
into those yoric waters

it is, somewhat, like the first cast of spring
but also, like the last cast
    (of the year)
like the jaded cast of an old lover
but with the eternal vitality that love brings
with and without anticipation, this cast glides outward,
overward, onward, downward, forward, curveward,
floatward –
and the fish comes flyward, taking and flying skyward
then underwaterward
familiar and alien
    i and it
connected by a thread
renew and refresh
but with a knew perspective
    or perhaps i just see it that way –
my heart comes alive in my throat, relaxing me
and my meaning becomes clear to me
    all i can think is:
it's about time.

October 19

this is one of those days
    i try not to think
just flow
i do not fish, but contemplate
    which can be done at the same time
unless i have reason not to
    which there is today
do you know how to contemplate
    without thinking?
it is the most simple thing
    and can be done
with a minimum of superhuman effort
just let go of words and think about the
    qualities of the thing
not the notion that tree bark is rough

         but how it feels/smells/tastes/sounds/looks
see how much more there is to understand
         once beyond the words?
so take your meanings where you find them
and apply understanding
and whether or not you get this from me
         it is important that you get it
and you are free to do with it what you will
         think about it.

October 20

fall fishing is fun
autumn angling is all-encompassing
postsummer piscatory is pleasurable
diurnal dowaging is durable
vernal valor is verifiable
equinoctic excitement is exhilarating

so go
now
fish
do
be

cast your senses to the four winds
         or to the four elements
which by now include
         (do i need to spell it out?)
         air = air
         water = water
         earth = earth
and   fire = fire

that's pretty straightforward, right?
because it is just that simple
and universal

    which is how the iconoclastic fisherpoet
        sees self
most of the time, anyway.
the rest of the time . . .

    well,
what you see/hear/taste/smell/feel
        is what you get.
make of that what you will.

October 21

so –
what do you think, now?
have i learnt anything?
or do i just look at old things in a new way?
and does that mean me?
or am i asking the wrong person?
should i just look to myself?
should you?
do you expect me to have answers?
or to give answers?
or to wait for an answer?
  . . .

i could advice you
but free advise is worth the prise
see for yerself, then you ask the questions
i know now how little i know
and what a singularly wonderful feeling
to have come this far
still standing
still intact
healed
not as sure, but surer than before

i dont know where to find the answers
i dont know all the questions

i dont need to know these things
as long as
i know
> where to go
> to find the questions.

October 22

this day, worth noting, is special
a celebration is in order
i think to recognize it and you
through small ritual
not grand but significant
many things pinpoint their beginnings
from such a day
and truly, i do
let this be a simple celebration
with singing of song
and perhaps a fishing trip
to commemorate and mark

would you remember the time
out on the point
when a cottonmouth coiled round your rock
or late nite card games
or the hook that got me?
how about the boat that burnt
and the bluff from which
> one of us fell
not cognizant of being on the edge?

you know –
the amazing thing is that any of us
> could be here at all
how quickly a twisting fate
> alters completely and forever
there are so many traps and turns
> along the way

    that i am in utter and resolute amazedness
        at being anywhere at all
but i am here
who do i send the card to
i feel that something like that
        is in order.

October 23

thus begins my last fishing trip
        of the year
it is a week-long
        give or take
i fish or not, as mood dictates
sometimes from need
        or want
        or whatever
just because.

there is a feeling of poignancy
        to the last trip
the constant realization that
        each trout may be the last
but that is a reminder that should be carried
        at all times
not just at an arbitrary ending of a season

this is something i have learned
        in part
from the red setter
        who enjoys
each moment
        and lives it fully
without words
        but with meaning

at this time
        each cast takes on more implication

on this trip
        each trout becomes more vividly etched
now
        the ticking of time becomes louder
in the moment
        i fish
and the red setter does what he does
        a boon companion.

October 24

i travel lighter now –
there is no need to stuff the vest
with the toolery to meet all seasons
i have the basics
        leaders, hemostat, oils, and knife
and a box of adamses
        in various sizes and forms
and i have
        a hat and waders
and, of course, my favorite fly rod
it is a lighter rod and more delicate in approach
it casts effortlessly and smoothly
and the line settles to the water like a leaf
with scarce a ripple

these trouts –
        browns, bows, and hybrids
feed to store fat for winter
i release them, noting the vividness of hue
        the buildup of tissue
        and the golden spark of eye
each is a story, but i cant tell you them all
        go
        and catch
        go
        and fish
        go

and find
yours.

October 25

Journal Entry:

Today I fished the upper reaches of the spring branch.I started below the falls near the bridge and worked my way up.I didn't see fish rising, so I found a brown woolly nymph in my hat band and fished the edges of the main current.The takes were gentle but solid.The day was magnificent; the skies were intensely blue and clouds floated dreamily.A slight breeze occasionally stirred the branches.The water was very very clear and i could see most of the trout strike before i felt them.I caught a couple under the bridge, one under the falls, and picked up several as I worked toward the spring.A muskrat swam from the reeds and circled around me before heading downstream.I moved past that stretch and fished a calm pool where the stream broadened.It was there that I spotted the broad flash of a large nymphing trout.It took several minutes of egg-walking to get into position for a cast, but I finally did.I lost count of the casts, but there must have been at least twenty.The trick was to get the fly on the left side of the fish about six inches off the streambed.It turned several times before finally taking.What a fight!For a large trout, it leapt and danced like a ballerina.Its stamina was unbelievable and at times I felt that the hook would wear itself out.Finally I landed the fish and admired its muscle and spirit and then released it.A most joyous occasion for this time in the season; hope springs eternal, but the reality of realities is that it is harder to maintain it this late in the season.

October 26

it rained today

thunder and lightning gave me cause to pause
it cannot be prudent to wave
      an eight-foot graphite rod
      toward the heavens
      in an electrical storm
so i stayed in the cabin and read
i didn't stay with one book very long
but read favored excerpts from old friends

i came to the realization that each
      had a favored spot
      a spring branch
      a personal well
that centered all experience

funny –
i never saw that before
at least, not in that way

they all seemed so well-traveled
that i thought they perpetually sought
      new places
but not so –
they each sought a shangri-la
suggested by a personal fave
but never fully realized
now i understand
      (or rather, accept)
the best spot is the one
      that seeks me out
      and opens itself to me
      one i can love
      warts and all

October 27

ANGLATOR: You should have a reasonable perspective on things now. I have taught you what little

	I know, and now the rest is up to you. Do you have any questions or doubts that I might assuage?
SPORTSTOR:	You read my mind . . . again. I should expect that by now. Yes, I would like to know if there is much more to learn, since you have brought us to a point of acceptance; do we still seek other perspectives?
ANGLATOR:	That is for you to know, and I believe you already do. Total comfort is the lack of motivation. Some doubt and unsurety will help you grow. Growth will lead to learning and learning to awareness of how little you know. I started by learning all I thought there was about fishing and soon learned that I did not know anything at all. Each passing day brings more evidence of things I do not know. I accept this and revel in it.
METAPHOR:	So acceptance is like . . .
ANGLATOR:	Excuse me, it just is what it is and no more than that. It is enough.
SPORTSTOR:	So I accept my questioning.
ANGLATOR:	Good – that will be enough.
METAPHOR:	And I accept all things that a thing is.
ANGLATOR:	Good – that will be enough.

October 28

no large fish today
    (no small ones either)
no great numbers of fish
    (but not skunked either)
just fishing –
    instead of relinquishing
    to portentous fate
i could describe it, but
    what would be the point to that?

if you have been paying attention
        then you know
if you have gone then you know
        if you can see then you can see –
so i now compress
and let the meaning reside in the words
and all of the explanation and description
should already have
        clarified rarified distilled it for you
eh?
you know what it was/is/will be
without the particulars
which, by the by, are merely
        supportive circumstantial evidence –
        anyway.
so . . .
here's all you need to know
about this particular day:
        i went fishing.
               comme il faut

October 29

so there you have it
what to do with time
and energy
and whatever you have
        in whatever proportions you have
this day is another
i could fish or not
because all moments have their golden hue
invisible till looked at
        to answer the eternal existential riddle.
this speaks to me and i to it
without conversation
        words, that is –
and i remember the thoughts conveyed
by all of it

                    from the spirits of the water
                        to the red setter
        as i heard it.
        and i understand that it is impossible
                    to fish
with an albatross round my neck.
besides the fact that it interferes with my casting,
            it just plain looks silly
                when i see my reflection
                in the waters.

October 30

today will be my last outing for this season –
        true, the season does not officially close
        until tomorrow, but i hate to
        relinquish my choice to that of arbitrarity
actually, i could fish catch-and-release
        during the off-season, but
ironically,
        i fish and release during the season
my reason for observing this day is that
        it is part of a cycle
        and it must have some sort of closure
        it must stop to begin
        it must have form
i just happen to think it is arbitrary
        but most things are
unless they are not . . .

so i fish this last day
knowing that each trout may be
        the last for a while
which is (relatively speaking, of course)
        always the best way to think.
the setter knows and seems meditative
as he sits on a boulder overlooking my efforts.
the trout come to me

        as they usually do
in varying numbers and sizes and frequency
it is what makes this life infinitely wondrous
        as does magic
        and love
        and birth
        and life . . .
so the closing of the season looms
and i fish
        slowly
        thoughtfully
        without words
        with innocence
on the spring branch.

October 31

all hallow's eve
and strange creatures walk the earth
desiring to catch just one more trout
before the season closes
for another year

hay is bundled into gigantic misshapen silhouettes
barely visible in the morning sun
lending a sense of doom
to the tans brouns and oranges
of the already harvested landscape

the soon-to-be-near-dormant trout
will not sleep
but will be alive in the frigid waters
gathering what they can with impunity
trying to survive until spring

but on this last day
as they, like the grizzlies and the woodchucks,
store up energy in fat cells

they are liable to make one more mistake this year
and mistake an imitative or impressionistic item for the
THING

and learn (or remember)
just exactly what the hook is like
and find themselves locked in
what they perceive
as yet another struggle to survive

November

November 1

the elventh month
time to pack away the gear and reflect
the colors of fall have faded to grays and browns
the electricity of anticipation has grounded
rods are cased
the vest slumps on a peg
waders are hung upsidedown
and the net is wrapped and hung

a wordless eulogy accompanies this storing of life
and only brief reflection passes
to acknowledge the importance of each piece
and here it will rest until a fidgety winter day
when it is brought out for inventory
and repair
and deeper reflection
and only the flychest
with its ostrich plumes
and stork and pheasant feathers
and badger fur and sheep's wool yarn
and threads and hooks
and tools
will see service until the spring
but not today
because the realization that the options have lessened
gives rise to inactivity
or, at least, to activity that has been put off
like fixing a door or window
or cleaning out the fishing truck
or just plain pre-fidgeting

November 2

And then the memories begin coming back
like conventioneers – more every year

each with a "hello I'm . . ." tag
and ready to introduce another

the mind goes back to the spring branch
and fast forwards past the first fishless days
altho they are acknowledged
to the first one

a mentor stood by my side offering the word
i tried but could never seem to get it all to happen
        at the same time
we stood in the frigid current, he in waders – me in levis
        and i tried

the long rod was half again as tall as me
and the line was an equal length
the leader was another equal length
and keeping the rhythm necessary for levitating all of this
        at once
and still not tangling the line
or snapping off the fly
or hooking my own ear
took so much effort that it seemed near impossible
to think about where in the current the lure would land

but eventually it happened in one of those zen moments
when I forgot to think about trying to accomplish
and all I did was DO
and it happened
and the fish struck with a tentative bump
and I snapped back the rod
and felt the solid throbbing live essence
and the fish leapt
and my mouth fell open
and finally it came to my net
wordlessly I shook and turned toward the bank
and I said "i caught a trout"

and my mentor said
>"there's a hook in both ends of that line, boy"

November 3

And in my yallow couth
I logged the fish date time weather lure conditions
 location impressions
and mumbers nattered
after the first
and I kept that log until the tally reached ten-thousand
fishes i had brought to bank
until i had a vision
of fig bish
and embraced the fever of obsession
in the awareness that size not numbers mattered
and i fished deeper in the pool
and in another zen moment caught one
one that was a mere ounce less than testimonial size
but close enough to fire me with realization of the possibility
and i became a heron
wading in the shallows but peering into the depths
looking not for just any lie
but for the best lie of the pool
for there the fittest survive
and drive away all those less fit
and i preyed upon those places
disdaining lesser fish
until the day i found it worked it skipped lunch
 worked it some more and finally . . .
"thar she blows"
and under the bridge where i had logged so many fish
i found one that had been there all the time
waiting
disdaining my lures until i had delivered the one specified
 for her alone
and she accepted it
and i never saw the bridge hole the same again

November 4

other-than-trout-memories come back to me

like the day on Sakakawea when four of us
man brother son and me
trolled from a boat for walleye
often through swimming areas
where bikini-clad nymphets stood indignantly
to inform us that we were in the wrong place
"depends" we told them
"on what you think we're looking for"
and we trolled on
and caught northerns on spinners
and northerns on plugs
and then I thought I should try a Big-O
       you know
one of those Arkansas bass plugs
like nothing these northers and wallys had ever seen
and as we passed the scoria again she hit
like 2,000 pounds of kilned clay building material
and I landed her
not easy – she was big and strong, but I did
too pretty to filet, I wanted to bring her back home
and I did in spite of
truck transmissions burning out – renting an overpriced
pickup on a Sunday – skipping sleep – finding new ice often
– asking a chef to keep her on ice for me – and then finding
her as a centerpiece on the salad bar – finally getting her
home – and trading guitar work for a skilled worker to
preserve her likeness –
and she is still with me to bring back those days
of comradeship and adventure
in a ship on the low seas
and I thank her spirit
for adding to mine

November 5

And now, when the seeking of BIG fish has been relegated
to those needful of such
PARTICULAR fish stand out
like the she-bass who busted a popper at dusk
as I stood on the dock of the mushroom house
actually trying to catch bluegills
like a boy, but with a long rod

I cast toward the swirl and she took
and I thrilled to the sudden feel of the weight of a GOOD
fish
she tried several times to defy gravity (and me)
by launching herself heavenwards
and suspending herself
and time
briefly

and
for me
she will always be in that suspended moment
in the air
reflecting the twilight
spraying the water in oblong droplets
above the earth

altho where she truly is today
i cannot say
because, after brief admiration
i released her gently into the water
unhooked and free

and i wondered if it were she
that I later saw walloping a water snake
as orca would a seal
i said she was not big
but maybe that was only relatively so . . .

November 6

And I remember once
me and the red setter went fishing
for just anything
he seem confused that i could release a fish
after trying so hard to catch it
and
wanting to share the experience with me
would submerge his head and blow bubbles from his nose
and try to track the trout to its lair
but he found he could not blow bubbles
and sniff at the same time
he could still try, tho
we shared that

and so one day –
i cast a plug in a river pond
one of those neither this nor that places
near a dakota town of water
and i would have been content with any bass or other
and would have remembered the day any way

but i saw the swirl along the edge of the school of bluegill
and cast
and watched
dumbly
numbly
as these great jaws opened like a scoop
and lurched toward the floating big-o

    and nailed it

    epic battle – no wire leader – cautious – strong –
    running – give line – keep up the pressure – wide-
    eyed (me & the setter & the fish) – starting anew
    every time it seemed over –
    finally rolling over

but I had no net and had to do what i could with what i had
so I waded into the river pond and directed that
      great northern
to between me and the shorebank
and lofted it with a boot skyward
it landed in the long grass

measured in feet rather than inches
its head nearly dwarfed that of the setter
who seemed amazed
considering my usual catches
and who seemed fascinated by the toothy mouth
especially when it popped its jaws in defiance

November 7

But
it is not always the catching that makes the day memorable
I remember my father waiting for drifting crappie to find us
and taking me to first smaller creeks and ponds
then rivers and lakes

and helping me
teaching me
guiding me
in my pursuits

but always able to get up earlier in the morning
and already have coffee and eggs and bacon ready
how did he know all that STUFF then
had he been guided as well

or did he draw upon more universal things
and just KNOW what was what
or did he just make enough trips to the well
to appreciate the water

did he engender this respect in me for nature

or did he just let it happen
the way he let me respect him –
he expecting but never demanding

our cycles intersected too briefly

November 8

I can remember
the good and the bad
and sometimes I can not forget
tho i need to

but i can get lost in the simplicity of woodcraft
and fry beans and chili
over a fire
and the crackle of the branches
intermingles with the sputtering in the pan
and wailing of coyotes
and the chirruping of cicadas

and
like nick
i can take to the woods to
remember-forget
what i need to
as he did on the big two-hearted
or was it really the fox
because sometimes the literal
gets lost in the literary
making a truth truer than the real

but like nick
i know that sometimes i want to stay in the clear current
and lose myself in the simplemindedness of repeated chore
and leave the swamp to fish on other days because

like nick

i have wounds that slow me in the swamp
and i have learned to sleep with the light off
and like nick i can coexist as the man and the boy
altho within myself rather than in text

but like nick's son i ask
why do people have to die, daddy
?

November 9

and the answer in the wind is that cycles within cycles must play themselves out
and that cycle is independent albeit interdependent of other cycles
and each
in its turn
must follow the proscribed PATH
toward
WHAT?
fate destiny completion fulfillment epiphany epitome
descent into the underworld
dust to dust
glory in the highest
or possibly recycling
altho it irks me to think
that a soda can
can live more lives than I

or anyone for that matter

but i find solace in the fact that my cycle of usefulness
perhaps
has more purpose than the can
and allow myself the egotistical perspective that
my cycle has more quality
than
one so unlucky as to never be able to fish

or to ever know why

November 10

Did I ever tell you the one about me and TS and the skunk?
No?
Well, here then –
me & TS went fishing.
and we caught some and cooked them over a fire
next to a lean-to
up the hill
from the spring branch

and he thought i disposed of the bones and viscera
and i thought he . . .
but no
and after a time
of good conversation and beer we slept
soundly
or at least i did
because
sometime during the night a skunk decided to share our windfall
and our fire and quite possibly considered the lean-to
but settled by our feet munching complacently
just loud enough to wake TS
not me
i slept the sleep of the innocent deeply deeply dreaming
and snoring suddenly
alerting the skunk and TS
who both went on guard
TS later said that he wondered if it might not be
    worth the risk to make the sudden move
of slitting my throat as a sacrifice to the skunk
hopefully to avoid being sprayed
and to indicate his good will toward the skunk
as fate would have it i rolled over and stopped snoring
and the skunk locked eyes with TS
for what may have seemed an eternity

but for reasons of his own
finished his snack and left leisurely
i slept well
never dreaming

November 11

When the papers were signed
did anyone know that
this was not the war to end all wars
that it would happen again

well, i suppose not

but it did

and then
failing to learn from mistakes
the world created new and better ways
to destroy all life on the planet
take that you violent warmongers:
if you insist on being warlike
we will blow you up

but i did realize
as i signed my papers
that an armistice only calls off
the overt hostilities
and that the problems that were not solved in war
if merely shelvd
can arise anew

the only way to solve a problem is to solve the problem
and to recognize that the problem always resides in self
not other
and that self is the only fixer of the self

i never throw anything away

thinking that it can be fixed
and may have life left

i didn't want to be thrown away either
i wanted to fix me but . . . ah, well –

i suppose i have more time to go fishing now
and that is where i can fix me the best
and find a separate armistice

November 12

fishing fixes me
and sometimes catching is the thing
after my surgery
when i had pain
and could only sit in the ragged green chair
and identify canadian woodpeckers stopping by the feeder
      on their way south
i had to find part of me that worked

and so

i gathered up my tackle – the light stuff (for panfish)
      and set out for a pond
with two (2) canes, one to take the place of each leg at times
and as i fished for the bluegill i leaned on one cane
      and kept most of my weight
on my best leg – the one with less nerve damage

and i cast

and caught bluegill and felt . . . well, better for just being out
it was cold though
and i cast toward a swirl and could not believe . . .
that a monster bass inhaled the lure
      and bolted for other shores
with my light tackle all i could do was follow

        and keep pressure
one
painful
step
at
a
time

and around the pond we went, she always in charge
and me following keeping up the pressure
and bearing the pain

and almost back to where we started she tired and turned
        and i eased her toward me
i couldn't bend to grasp her
so i took a step backwards and let the canes fall
and i fell forward on the bank – free hand outstretched
and grabbed her lower jaw in that grip that circumvents
struggling
and brought her to me

only because the pond was due to be drained and because i
knew she would perish
did i choose to keep her
        and through the art of a trained craftsman
her likeness resides upon my wall to remind me that i had
come close to giving up
but that it is always worthwhile – to bear the pain

November 13

Did i tell you the one about . . .
the friend who said we must fish the pond
altho it is small, it is overpopulated
and needs to be fished to reduce the number
to make better habitat for the ones left
who will have room and resources to grow
and fishing i saw the swirl

and reached for the other rod
and cast a big-o lure
past the swirl
to the reeds
for that is the best approach to a lie
in that place

and she took

she was large, larger by far than those i had considered
wallhangings but
when i landed her i paused
i knew what the pond needed
and she was of course that what

and so, altho we had our good intentions
for improving the habitat
nature had already seen the problem
formulated the solution
and given this voracious predator
sustenance to grow to a size
through which she could
reduce the overpopulation
without our effort

and i released her
to do what she needed
with perhaps little
of our humble assistance

November 14

there was one trout...
lithe and colorful, she came to me
i found she measured well
and another might have kept her
i thought her place to be in the river
and so released her

if the catching is the thing
then a trophy is not necessary
in the scheme of things
and dragging one from the river
to show people in town
obscures the meaning

when i return to town without fish
some think i had no luck
or am just plain silly.
as long as i know better
then things are as they should be
and i am the better for it

they have to answer to their demons
or the sad lack of them
i go fishing for whatever
whenever i can
and carry with me the memories
of just that very thing

November 15

when i was a kid,
        things were different –
all things were possible
        (relatively speaking, of course)
and the world was my . . .well,
        oyster
        playground
        cup of tea
        domain
        universe
        destination
        pearl
but i focused
        on a few things

not knowing
> how they fit together

it took time to
> figure it out

so then i understood focus
and understood what it is
> that i do –

i like to think
i like to work with my hands
> somehow, it seems
> that i never got past this

everything i do contains these elements

i like to work with writing and reading
> thinking and turning pages

i like to play music
> thinking and striking chords

i like to pet the red setter's head
> when he lays it on my knee

I like to fish
> solving problems, tying flies
> casting, catching (sometimes)

i like to walk holding hands
> with the one who cares
> dreaming
> along the spring branch

now that i know
> i know what matters

and i know why i remember.

November 16

i remember when the red setter was a pup. he stood out from the litter with his unique markings – white chest-blaze, white stockings, white muzzle, and white tip-of-tail. and when i knelt on the floor to pick a pup and called, he was the one who came to me without hesitation, as though he knew, somehow, that there would be or already was a bond between us. and i took him home to be with me forever and named him for an author, an old friend through the letters who possessed all the good qualities a writer needs. like this pup. we saw the ocean and the mountains for the first time together and traveled the country in an all-american red ford pickup. he, like i, felt that the windshield of that truck offered the best vantage to observe the trek west. and back again. our wordless communication reached a point of understanding some years back when i misguidedly took him to an obedience class. the instructor informed me that this dog would not now not ever respond to command and that if he did anything i told him to it was just because he wanted to do it. and so we came to terms. and he did the things i wanted him to do at times. because he wanted to please me. so i, understanding now, treated him likewise, and we went down roads side by side. we discovered shared likes, oh like oreos and summer sausage and sleeping in on a rainy day and resting by a crackling fire when the snows blow. and more. i remember those things we saw and did together and smile to watch him curled by the fire, white turned to grey and the white tip-of-tail lost in some or the other incident involving a door and at the catscar on his eyelid – close call – and watch him dream. i wonder if his dreams take him to those places we traveled and to happy memories of times gone by. he seems content in his autumn years to reflect and doze. but now he stirs and nuzzles my hand, wanting to go outside for a while. i open the door for him, altho he can open it for himself, as he taught me years ago, and he runs in the snow making tracks, scooping it with his nose and rolling in it to create setter-shaped snow angels. then he comes back to the door and scratches as tho to come back in but wont when i open it. understanding, i join him and we walk the path along the spring branch sharing.

November 17

as i put away the tackle
on the closet shelf
i find a box
containing a bundle of letters
from various and sundry personages
exigent in my past
people who cared about me
one way or another
who wrote me
to let me know
so that i could keep the letters
and always remember that

some of the senders write no more
for reasons beyond their control
some no longer write to anyone
others have other reasons
but still –
at one time, these thoughts
were put to paper
to be kept
and read
later –
perhaps: now.

these do not make me sad
over missing the senders;
i am glad to ever have known them at all
and glad they felt like writing
do you get my drift?

November 18

Dear Tony,

I hope things are going well for you. I know you have been busy, so I haven't dropped by. I didn't want you to think that I had not thought about you so I decided to write and let you know a few things. First, I did not want to leave, but I had no choice in the matter. The situation I was in caused me to go without being able to talk to you in any detail. It had nothing to do with you – you are a good person and it is obvious you care about the people around you. You have never done any harm to anyone that I know of and have only the best of intentions and hopes for others. I am sure you understand that I did not want to cause you any sorrow, but events unfolded that took things out of my hands. If you ever think of me, I hope it is with fond memory of the time we had together and is tempered by the knowledge that I really did (and do) care about you. My favorite memory of you is of the time we walked along the spring branch with the red setter and just talked about what makes that a special place. When you go there again, please think of me and know that I am glad to have known you. Take care. All the best.

Say hello for me.

Yours,
  (name blurred)

November 19

if you were superstitious,
you might have some sort of feeling
about the number nineteen
it seems to come up at various times
in significant contexts
i dont know that it portunes good or bad

but it does seem connected to
    life experiences
    those which alter
what is it makes the difference?
you know, between it and another?
fate, maybe
or, just possibly,
a psychological overlay
of unconscious communication
imposing a pattern of significance
through an emotional umbrella
    or
maybe not.
who knows?
i have come to believe
that the only inherent significance
of any one thing is
that which we attach to it
this is why i keep "sakes"
to remind me of those and then
and not as fetish or totem –
numbers, in all likelihood,
are just keepsakes of luck
    or the lack of it.

November 20

so i have an idea of how
my world fits me
but i am not sure
how i fit into the world around me.
i fish, therefore i am.
i poeticize, therefore i ram-ble
i write, therefore aye think i am
    it is a muddle at times,

(not the pome – it is from the heart
    not the brain; its muddliness

                is inherent. i mean life.)
a good deal of it is
          out of my control
          or yours
it requires reaction to action
and action to affirm
perhaps my purpose is
          as a scribe
to note that
          the more things change
          the more they dont
life is unique in its sameness
and in the fact that so few
ever recognize this or
know that it is ever the same
          in its uniqueness
its all just –
          perspective
isnt it?

November 21

i dont read newspapers regularly
and when i do, i generally skim them
for the big picture

you know –
          the comics
          the fishing report
          names that i know
          changes in places

i am the same way about the radio
i listen to:
          music
          humor
          talk
          stuff that catches my attention

and i watch very little TV
    movies
    and glimpses of stuff

i read books
and talk
and look
and observe
and think
i guess it boils down to this:
    i dont know exactly what goes on
    in a specific sense
    but i have some solid ideas
    about understanding
    when something happens
whether or not i like it.

November 22

do you understand
that altho a man died on this day
it was not the man who was mourned
except of course by those who knew and loved him
what fell that day was
the thing that should never
under any circumstances
be taken away:
    hope
and the days that followed
presented others who could lead
but none who could offer
    hope
of camelot revisited
and the answers then so far away
seem no closer today

the choice seems to be
to find it and them

within the self
and the pursuit
of happiness
because
quite possibly
hope and trust were misplaced
if ever embodied
in another
or in an institution
which by definition
have other agenda to support
and who
after all
dont know you or me
as i did not know the man
who fell
but i did know
      hope

November 23

but what brings it all home
for me anyway
is when i get phoned or visited by friends
who tell me that a pronouncement has been made
and only a specified number of days begins
and hope has passed away
but i cant convince them
that i too have a specified number of days
kept as a secret
and that what matters is not the numbers
but what is done with those days
and it will be done for each of us in our time
so
i try

i dont know what it is like to live under such a sentence
but i do know that i learned to appreciate the day

when i ran
like jesse james
because a bogus signer of a bogus warrant
decided that would serve his purpose
and the caves and woods served
as they did for jesse
until i made the border
and eventually my continued freedom was assured
and they unsigned the paper
because they can do that
among other things
about all i learned from them was that they believe who tells first
not best not truest
but what i did learn is that each day can be the last
and must be lived
and that to BE
and to DO
are processes
not goals

November 24

i took some time
to attend a play
a thing of interest,
but interpretative in nature.
the setting paid abeyance
to the ideas of unities
of time and place
       and
characterization was rich
i found that in this new form of drama
       audience is participant
and my lines were spontaneous
       no chance for rehearsal
and no pronouncement on
       whether right or wrong

no second takes

it was just the way it was
        and it happened that way
as it should and will

some of the players thought that
        they had a script
but when they read between the lines
they found out that there was space
        to be filled in

the first act, then, was tenuous
without proscription or dialectic
        just a few stage directions
intermission did not help
        the second act was the same
but offered a little more insight
a second intermission did not help
        the third act was where
        things came together
and the patterns became apparent
and the characterizations became complete
and the degrees could be seen to which
        the play conformed to
the precepts of
        comedy
        or
        tragedy

November 25

so on this day, as you probably guessed,
i find myself thankful
for those things which i have and for those
        friends who helped
(about fifty of them at last count,
        though the numbers are apparently dwindling)

and mostly because i can still continue somehow
and now and then return to the spring branch

***

THANKS!

****

what more needs be said?

November 26

one of my fondest recollections
is of a day when
      i fished
several of us had gone up the spring branch
looking for unique trouts
hunting like hawks
climbing for a better vantage
      we found one that was almost impossible to catch
it lay under a downed willow
on the downstream side
no cast could reach it from the opposite side
dapping from the bluffside would preclude landing it
one of us waded as close as possible
while the others directed casting
      artillery style
we watched casts inch their way
toward the food lane of this secluded fish
the casts were long, but accurate
before long one cast was perfect
      the trout took
the caster, chest deep already, stepped forward
      and walked off the ledge
only the arched rod was raised from the surface
      but the line was taught

he raised his head as he regained his senses in the current
and found the trout attached – also heading downstream
the rest of us followed the struggle
ready to jump in if necessary
but the battle came to a calm pool
and was concluded
we all felt part of the accomplishment
        without the various perspectives
a unique experience might have been missed.

November 27

another time –
we launched canoes in a far northern lake
just fishing
        not for anything in particular
the day was damp and cool
        but bearable
we watched loon and moose
        and caught fish
        from various contexts
one of us, a photographer, clicked pictures
another, an artist, sketched
yet another, a chef, created a shore lunch
and another, a writer, made notes
        we all paddled
        and we all caught fish
        we all saw things
        and helped with dishes
– and we all made memories –
        but each one unique.

i heard the loon call
and the moose grunt
i saw the northern wilderness
in its undisturbed beauty
and it all was made more memorable
from having been shared

even though
each of us
saw and heard and felt,
 smelled and touched
different experiences simultaneously
 and still carry
differing memories.

November 28

snow is confirmation
it is indeed going to be winter now
i sit in the cabin with the red setter
and look over tackle catalogs
the fire blazes its muscles
and warms the sleeping dog
and the pondering man
and coffee warms my insides
and the steam drifts into dream

i dont order as much as i wish for
there is only so much time to use it
and some wont work for me
and some is too expensive
 (for my wallet
 not my wishes)
but, then –
i really dont need all of it
some of it is just lure
and tries to convince me of its necessity
still, it doesn't hurt to look.

i stack the catalogs
 along with magazines
 books
 legal pads
 and stuff
and gaze into the fire

    primaeval flyfishermen never knew
        what they were missing
but they still fished
       (altho they probably wished)
i move the plane of my thinking
and wish for good things
     . not in the catalog
and understand that this is part of it
so,
even with the snow falling
and the temperatures dropping
i find that which i truly need –
      hope.

November 29

ANGLATOR: ...

SPORTSTOR: Why do you sit so quietly by the fire? Is it some strange melancholy that has overtaken you? I have never seen you so quiet. You have cleaned the tackle and put it away. Has this made you sad? Are you pensive on the loss of fishing weather or do other demons plague you?

ANGLATOR: No ... no. I am happy in my recollection of a fine season. My outward silence is mute witness to an inward joy. There are things yet to be done, but first there is the remembrance of a good season with good companions and the sorting of detail to make sure that nothing is lost.

SPORTSTOR: That is good, but you had me worried for a moment.

ANGLATOR: Oh, there are always things to worry about, but they cannot intrude upon the fishing. It is good to know that each time the tackle is put away may be the last time it is used. Whatever we have experienced may be the

SPORTSTOR: sum and total of what we will have. That is why it must be nurtured and protected during the doing.
SPORTSTOR: And that is a happy thought?
ANGLATOR: The happiness comes not from what we might miss but from what we did not miss. That is inward and is the warm core of my being. The quiet is simply to enhance reflection. Notice that a still pool reflects more clearly than a shallow riffle.
METAPHOR: Now that is an idea that I can relate to. I am the thing I do; I do the thing that I am. And, at the same time, I am something completely different.
SPORTSTOR: But I like to think about the coming season and of the new experiences that await.
ANGLATOR: That is good and worthwhile, but remember that it is addition to what you already have, which is considerable.
METAPHOR: A foundation to build upon.
SPORTSTOR: A start.
ANGLATOR: A complete experience.
METAPHOR: One turn of the wheel.
SPORTSTOR: Cycle.
ANGLATOR: Yes . . .

November 30

ever been to an auction?
i went to one that moved me –
it was an estate
        actually of the wife of a doctor
        who had passed away long before
she had kept his things for years
        fly rods and reels
        books
        paintings
        carved wooden figures

       stuff
        & paraphernalia
i think i would have liked him
although i never met him
or even knew who he was
but the stuff he left
told about him
his books colored the picture
the pictures colored the moods
and he seemed a good soul

i had to pause
was this what it came to?
this stuff being bid on
by people who didn't really know him?
i would rather think
that they were going to get some
       of his good memories
by possessing his things
otherwise, why bother?
a fly rod is just the middle connection
       between man and trout
and only becomes significant
when one or the other is in contact
perhaps a book can serve the same purpose
       as a link – soul to soul
so i bid on
       just one
it was not a big nor famous book,
but it carried the link
i was outbid

       but that is as it should be
i formed my link
and the line is in the pome.

December

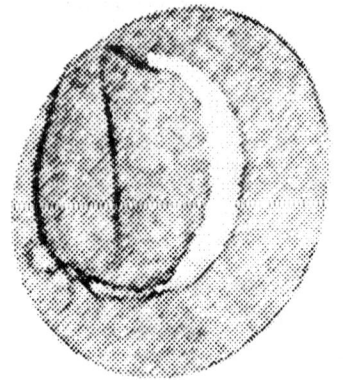

December 1

is this the beginning of the end?
where does it go from here?
as it comes to a close – does it offer promise of continuation
is this truly the end point of the cycle or
just another point of an infinite set of points
      composing a geometric figure
whose shape is only apparent from another perspective

or if the close of my cycle
do i end or transform
from a nymph to a larva to an adult
and am i now spentwing

no

there has to be more and i am now through
      enough of the cycle to see that
i find my purpose in directedness and belief and hope
and as i watch the land transform itself to shades of grey
I affirm my existence and acknowledge my share
      of other cycles

I celebrate birth and the potential fecundity
      of the now dormant life substance
I look forward to my place in heaven and
thank my creator for this chance
because that is exactly what I and all have or had –
      a chance
and whether or not got the winning number in the lottery
at least had a chance
unless not trusting to fate
and choosing a direction
and believing that there is a purpose to everything turn turn
and accepting and appreciating and loving those
      who love back
without judgement

amen
beam me up god.

December 2

some days i am so tired
even upon waking
i reach for glasses and reason
with fumbling fingers
disoriented i try to focus
to see if i am in an unfamiliar place
or if my own place has somehow become so
i want to be home
but i am not sure
it is a long time till the season
and the silence hurts
i make coffee
the aroma is reminiscent
but only fills an aspect of the void
i wonder if this is how it is
supposed to be
even before the first cup is down
i write
because this is how i clarify
i don't share those visions already concrete
but try to lassoo the amorphous
and now is the best time
when i can hold no biases
but manage to barely hold a cup
it is best at this time
when i have not yet met the world head on
and have just come from within myself
as i put the words on the page
they surprise me
as they should you on a first reading
but after i have done this
for me and for you
i feel more fit

and ready to face the world
and go home
which is, after all
the journey
and not
the place

December 3

the idea of
        cycle
confuses some folks
who think that the thing ends up
        right back where it started
                not so.
a cycle is three-, not two-
        dimensional (at least)
it could (relatively speaking, of course)
revolve around a single central point
and, at certain times, pass through
the same point
but everything would have to be perfectly proportioned
to form a sphere
        (highly unlikely)
a spiral could conceivably illustrate this
        but
if the dimension of the turn decreased
        then entropy would be observed
and that doesn't always apply
        no.
i conceive these cycles as following a similar bent
but revolving about a central point
        which itself moves
giving the impression of a shape
        like a non-shrinking spiral
or a circle which never meets its start
it looks like, if i may attempt to illustrate,
        a spring.

ok?

December 4

this vision of cycle does not,
        however,
encompass variation
which is, apparently, inherent
in all things –
        hence,
offshoots sometimes become
        the main core
otherwise,
we would all be in the same boat
a dangerous situation,
        if all are flyfishing
(too much line – too many hooks)
        so,
add to that image of spring
a diversive effect
sending out tendrils
at various junctures
themselves dividing further
and notice that the overall effect
is that the
        spring
will
        branch.
ok?

December 5

what is encompassed by this structure?
why, it is the core
        of being
        doing
and for each of us
        is different

yet much the same –

but how is the quality or correctness determined?
    by each of us
    being
    doing
    different things
still much the same –

    (in other words,)
there is no correctness involved
and quality is not the standard we must reach
but an overreaching of our own limitations
in whatever manner we choose.

isn't this too simple?
    of course –
it is as simple as a seed.
and as infinitely emergent
not to mention
    continuous.

December 6

and like that seed
i have grown to what i have become
at any point in the cycle
i, however, have glimpsed or divined
    my fate; mortality
and know that there are limitations
    that can not be overlooked
    (in a literal sense, that is)
but,
this is as it should be –
once a part, always a part
i will be in the core as legacy
in the same sense that my father was
and his father and so on

i can be found, after my time,
by reaching back
i will be seen through
what comes after me
        in my son and his
        in the things i have done
        in the minute changes i have wrought
perhaps, perhaps,
        in this pome, if it lasts.
altho that doesn't matter as much
        as my having written it
which was the point all along.
ok?

December 7

a day that will live in infamy . . .
how does a past sneak attack
        merit inclusion in memory?
probably as a reminder that
        we all lose sight of purpose
and may think that
        winning is everything
you know,
the idea that whoever has
        the most toys at the end
                wins.
i can not hold a grudge;
i let the bad feelings go
        and gain a perspective.
the point is
        that
i remember what happened
so that i can go forward
        but not blindly
i remember past human frailty and fault
        so as not to repeat it
i look to the future

    with an eye to the past
and live in the moment
     wherein all things converge

i offer my hand to you
    if you have fallen
because that is what friends are for
i use my energy to protect you
    rather than me
because it is likely
    that
you will go on
    when i am done
that,
    however vague,
is as much a purpose as there can be
ok?

December 8

the fisherpoet sits at the tying bench
adding wool and feathers to a hook
wrapping the thread with a whip finish
and putting a minute drop of cement on the knot

it is yet another adams
    not like the first one ever tied
    not like the last one
    not like many of the others
but still an adams

countless of these have been tied
    none like the others
    none identical to any other one
but all with similar characteristics and properties

what ends up being different
is what this one may do

the fisherpoet may cast it to a rising trout
and it may lure the trout
or it may snap off during a faulty cast
or snag in a tree.
then again,
it may never leave the fly box.
there is also the chance
that it will outlast the tier
and be found in the sorting of things
that occurs after the fact
what then?
will it be hidden in an attic trunk?
or framed on velvet and labeled?
or taken by another to the spring branch
      to be fished.
no way of knowing –
      just an observation.
and with that thought in mind,
      the fisherpoet ties another
sort of like the last,
      but not exactly,
knowing it will make a difference
      to a trout.
ok?

December 9

the tree branch serves in many ways
      beyond what it does for the tree
(and beyond the symbol, in a literal sense)
it becomes
      when appropriate
a staff
      for walking and wading
it gives the fisherpoet something to lean upon
      when legs alone are not enough
in that sense, it is yet one more friend
it has been used before

        to compensate for an injury
now it serves as support
        for the injury of age
the fisherpoet finds a way
to lean upon it while casting
        still keeping hands free
the riddle of the sphinx considered this
but forgot to mention what the man was doing
        that required him to walk on three
the point is
        that he must have had something to do
else he would have just let himself lie
the point is
        that there must be a point
we learned this in math –
        (the old math, i think)
        that there is an infinite number of points
        in a line
        or a circle
and while we dont have to identify any particular one
        we need to know that all are there.
so,   (in recent memory)
        the fisherpoet stands on three
casting to the rising trout
for what may be the last time
        with no other reason
than that is what he does
        until he can no longer.
ok?

December 10

does technology bear fruit?
        you bet!
on inception it is looking toward the future
in practice it is applied and error identified
with temperance it is a necessity

the fisherpoet adjusts trifocals
    to better see
        the knot
        the stream
        the sky
    and looks toward
        the past
        the future
        the present
    and employs a composite rod
        to cast better
        to cast easier
        to withstand the elements
and leans upon a composite staff
    to stand
    to walk
    to wade
and ties flies with the aid of
    a lighted magnifier on a mechanical arm
        because the eyes are much like the legs

and so it continues
    as best it can
in the cycle of things
and the fisherpoet
    even at this point in the cycle
remembers
    looks forward
        and casts in the moment.
ok?

December 11

the fisherpoet avoids the trap
that he sees others dive into
and that is the bitter angst of regret
for what was not done
or what will never be done

the fisherpoet now knows
that what was not done
was no more necessary than
    what was done
it was just more important
    to have done something.

and what will never be done
    is not under consideration
if it is essential
    someone will do it
some other fisherpoet
who draws from the past
and continues the cycle into the present
and leaves something for the next one

what serves it anyone to be bitter
    when it better serves anyone
        to be?

how wondrous to have been a part
    of anything at all
when so many never take the chance.

how sad
to have seen only pictures
to have heard only recordings
to have (how sad) only partaken of
    phosphor-dot images on a grid
to have listened to the tales
    with none to add
and to only realize this
    when it is too late.

the fisherpoet has known confusion, doubt, sadness and pain
    but only as a part of the overall picture.
ok?

December 12

so what?
so why?
so how?
so when?
so who?

doesnt matter
        unless you ascribe some special quality to any of
this

there are different ways to fish, you know –
some stand on the bank and do very nicely, thank you
some wade in the current and get along quite well
some employ a canoe or drift-boat
some sit on a pier or dock
some sit on a bridge
        there are different ways

what is important is for you to do something
        the best that can be done whenever you can
and that answers all questions

the fisherpoet has chosen one way
        and it has served him well
not only as a way to see
        but as a way to see being
it cannot be wrong
        if it is right for him

the companions who have shared
        have understood this
altho each in an individual manner
some still fish; others can no longer
        but once they all did
and each remembers that
        in one way or another

and each remembers the other
    in some way
and remembers the shared moments
    of understanding
even if that was only enacted
    as a passing wave or nod
on the spring branch
ok?

December 13

last night i remembered the sound of the cicada
i dont know why,
    but it came to mind
i wonder if i will hear it again
but if i dont, at least i can remember it
how appropriate, however
to think of one who spends so much of life
    in the dark
    underground
and only gets to emerge briefly
    to get a new perspective on things
even tho still following a basic plan

i remember when their cycle hit a peak
and they drowned out all other sound
they fell into water
and were devoured by erupting fishes
gorged, these fish disdained lures
but, at times, in a frenzy, engulfed indiscriminately

the same thing happened once with mayflies
and they were so numerous that
the skies looked snow-filled
at eighty degrees fahrenheit
so many fell
that the roads became slick

and snowplows were required to clear a path
in the scheme of things
few survive to long age
few get to fly for long
each had the chance, however
and some did fly and survive
until a time when they could no longer –
how could such a one
who had the chance
be bitter or regretful
considering the scheme of things?

December 14

i pulled a book from the shelf
which one doesnt matter
but i read into the night
and watched the story unfold
to its conclusion

i feel gratitude to the writer
for putting those things to paper
not because the answers were there
but because the writer asked questions
and then left me on my own.

the true starting point to anything
        that is worth doing
is a question; a problem; a conundrum
        a paradox
and no one person can formulate one of these
        alone
otherwise, each of us would continually be
        reinventing the wheel
        so to speak.
so i thank the writer and put the book away
for it is time for me to add to what i have taken
i have sown seed and put pen to paper

and sorted out the form to the questions
and asked a few myself

the trick (if it may be called that)
is to not be lured into answering the wrong question
long ago, i was asked:
> how many angels dance on the head of a pin?

first,
> the question involved "point" not "head"

significant, eh?
second,
> it was "pen" not "pin"

so:
> how many angels can dance on the point of a pen?

do you see how this could matter so much more to me?

December 15

i want just one more day . . .
oh, i know that i have philosophized overtly
about the way things are
and about how things are the way they should be
but,
> i still want just one more.

i accept my mortality
but i accept my humanity
and it is human
> to want just one more day

not necessarily for myself
> but just there for whatever

it wouldnt have to be a great day
or even a day to do something different
it could be just one more like any other
> with chance all its own

i would not be bitter if i knew
> that it could not be

i realize how few get this far

but that still doesnt stop me
>from wanting
>just one more

the view out my cabin window
>is snow
>and leafless branch
frost is on the edge of the pane
if i must contemplate this seeming need
then i will do so *in media res*
so,
>i put on
>long-johns
>thick socks
>a flannel shirt
>wool pants
>the worn boots
>a ragged sweater
>the stained coat
>the weathered hat
and i pick up the walking staff
and walk one more time
along the spring branch.

December 16

the fire wanes, occasionally devouring a throaty knot in an explosion of sparks. the restless feeling of wanting to do and complacency of wanting to be are eclipsed by the deeper chill that even the fire can not touch. the morning's duties finished, nothing remains to be said or done. and yet i can not sit still. the brown parka will not warm me but may protect me from the elements today, so i don it and reach for the hickory walking stick. its gnarled but polished surface grips my hand offering security against a sudden slip. gloves cover my hands and a hat rests on my head. the burgundy scarf hugs my throat and the old boots fit over two pairs of socks. i leave the cabin. and walk along the spring branch.

the greys and browns and stillness are relieved by an occasional glimpse of the splash of color of a wintering cardinal or the jerky hopping of a chick-a-dee. i pause to remember that this little bird is not even afraid of a bear – what a strong heart that tiny body must contain. walking on, i follow the path beside the stream and see little but the movement of the waters to signify life. what a cold desolate place even this can be at times. there is numbness in my feet despite extra socks and i need the stick to hold onto balance. after all the times i have walked this path it somehow seems unfamiliar and foreboding. even the sounds are cold – branches clattering the gurgle of the steamy waters reminding of their iciness yet i walk. at a bend in the stream near a bluff i see deer tracks telling who has passed this way. leading toward a sandbar are raccoon tracks. another day i might have followed them to learn their mystery but this day i walk. the hills seem higher and the path narrower. rocks seem to have come from nowhere to trip me but i go on. the path is longer than it was or maybe i miss the distraction of the obsession and the quest for the mystery. i walk on in greyness but my eyes follow the path rather than the waters. when i get to the grove it is still and i carry a stone from the bank to the mound, place it and turn to walk back alone – the quest completed. the red setter died today.

December 17

on different days,
      i write different things
some days i write poetry
      others . . .
well, i write other stuff
some days that would mean letters
so,
      i didnt write a pome today
i wrote letters
      another way of touching
but, (relatively speaking, of course)

        much the same.
if i wrote you a letter
        dont feel compelled to answer it
i understand that you are busy
and i didnt write it to instigate more work for you
i wrote to nod and wave in passing
what i mean is:
        if this letter moves you to do something
        then pass that along
        do something for someone else
i am complacent
        knowing what i know
        doing what i do
        being what i am
and having this day
        for what it is
i just wanted to let you know
        that i am fine.
        how are you?

December 18

i looked in the mirror this morning
        and wondered how i got so old
the thinned greyed thatch of hair
        shocked me
as did the grizzled beard
and
where did those wrinkles come from?
were they there yesterday?
i cant even count the scars
        inside and out
at this point
they healed in time
        but left reminders
and why do these dull pains
feel they have to tell me of
        changes in the weather?

    i can see for myself that
            things will be different.
    am i shorter now?
    it looks like it – but how did that happen?
    i dont remember anything that
            could have caused this.
    and why are my insides in rebellion?
            i used to be able to
              eat and drink as i saw fit.
    oh, well . . .
            how did i get so old?
    just lucky, i guess.

December 19

i found something in my desk drawer
i was just looking for a pencil
and there it was
it reminded me of a time long-gone
when i was full of it
without knowing what it was
i dont know if you would remember
but that doesnt matter
i do
so i stopped and thought about it
and was glad of the chance
both to have done
        and to have remembered
i never knew this was in the drawer
i suppose it was stuck way in the back
it may have gotten caught between the drawers
or somehow caught up in something else
it was such a simple thing to have triggered
        such contemplation
it was a cue
        opening the door to many memories
and it was such a simple thing.
        what was it?

ha!
      it was just
a slip of paper
a receipt
marked:
      "paid in full"
for the time we had
when we went someplace
      together.

December 20

i wrote today
i had something to say
what do you think?
was it worth the effort?
i trust you as a reader
knowing that you will be honest
      at least, with yourself.
if it isn't your cup of tea,
      then wait a while
      and give it a second chance
i wrote it with you in mind
      thinking that you might
           understand
there is not much i can do at this point
      (no regrets; there is much i have done)
but i can do this.
i can try to compress what i have learnt
      into something that
you can hold in your hand.
perhaps that will make it real for you
      it was already real for me
perhaps i can not tell you anything
      that you dont already know
but perhaps i can
      get you to see
      a difference

i hope you feel this was worthwhile
it was for me
and now i can put it on paper
      for you
and
      for me.

December 21

the shortest day of the year?
the cycles find an axis shift here, but why now?
why didn't THEY set up the calendar so that this day
      of the solar cycle
falls upon December 31?
it would make so much sense to end the year
      on the shortest day
and begin again with the daze getting longer
why didn't THEY ask me?
i would have told them.

but maybe they weren't paying attention anyway
and maybe they didn't care about that cycle
and maybe they were more interested in politics than in life
and maybe they wouldnt have understood
because there was not enough light on this day
or because gravity was working extremely well this day
and the relationship between those two has never been clear
      to me
except to accept that light has substance
and can be affected by gravity

and maybe the cycles within cycles only ask to continue
      and not to be correct.

December 22

i returned to the bridge
      to see and think

the water rushing under
reminded me of spring torrents
        but clearer
i saw trout working in the shadows
unaware of my presence
yet precautious, just in case –
they fed lightly
needing little to sustain them
        at this time of year
yet their cycles continued
unheeding yet intersecting my own
and even though these will not be caught
        by me, at least,
they affect me and move my blood
        heart to brain
        brain to heart
whatever goes on
        and i am glad to have seen them
because the point is not
        catching
it is fishing
        and this is part of it:
observing and understanding
accepting and rejoicing
being and doing
        being a part of it
letting it be a part of me.

December 23

well,
i didnt change the world
i didnt alter the cosmos
i didnt even get the fence painted
        before winter set in
that's ok . . .
        i didnt want to paint the fence, anyway
        i just thought i should

i did other stuff
and let go of what i couldnt do

i found some things
that were for me
and i find solace in all things
        however others see them
it all fits
    it all means
        something
you just have to look at it
    in the way that it was meant
    (which doesnt mean
        "in The Right Way")
is it too late to take a chance?
    never.
is it silly to think to change now?
    of course not.
is it meaningful to do something?
    always.

bear with me –
    i still have some things to share.

December 24

is it wise to follow a star?
to travel and seek?
to offer gifts?
to forget problems?
to be out of sync?

you tell me.

you will never know what could be
without what is
you will never know what is
without what was

you will never see
without looking
you will never find
without seeking

and it is all so simple
it is all there in whatever you do
if you are open to it
i touched the oak
and found its frailty
i held a dandelion
and felt its strength
i drank time
and swallowed space
i partook of now
and fed what will
join me
i have enough to share
and this blend of tea
can be brewed however you like
and i think you will find
it needs no sweetening
then, perhaps,
we can follow a star
      together
i think that would be wise.

December 25

I have a gift for you
it isnt much but i wanted you to have it
i wrapped it
as best i could
and filled in the card
so that you would know that it is for you
and i hope you like it

did you ever stand outside

in the new fallen snow
at midnight preceding this day?
i have
many times
and just a few minutes after the bell tolls
a calm sets in
like no other
at no other time of the year
and the animals seem to sense it
and relax
and look skyward
at the icily glittering points of light
which seem cumulatively to warm the soul
despite the winter cold
and the air breathed in is sweet
and the warmth comes from the inside out
and not a sound disturbs the still

and this wonderful feeling
informs without words
telling of magic on earth and in the heavens
tangible and real
and whispering
in a voice so low
that a candle could drown it out
that there is
hope.

December 26

is the gift the thing
        or is it the unwrapping
that makes it special?
or is it that it was freely offered
or that it was just for you?
i have received more than my share
        and have been grateful
both for the giving and receiving

i do not need further
but have more to give
i do not feel overwhelmed
but satiated
i do not feel regret
but . . .
      thankfulness
and it has been worthwhile
that was your gift to me
whether you know it or not
so,
thanks
and i hope that the new year
will bring all your hopes to fruition
it will, you know, if you let it.
if you do what you do
the best you can
and fish the spring branch
when the dogwoods bloom
and the redbuds flower –
so cast with anticipation.

December 27

the fisherpoet gathers his things
      sorts and packs
and puts them away
      carefully
for the day that they may be used again
the flies are safe in their boxes
the rods in their cases
leaders coiled and oiled
the waders aired and hung upsidedown
the books are on the shelves
the hat on the peg
the boots by the door
the pencils sit in a cracked cup

        on the desk
and the papers have been shuffled

enough wood has been gathered
to sustain the fire for
        however much longer it is needed
the cupboards contain food
and so the fisherpoet sits by the fire
alternately
        dozing
and
        dreaming
absorbing the warmth
and occasionally looking out the window
where a bright cardinal
        gathers nuts and berries
that were somehow overlooked til now
and the redbird sings of the spark
that maintains through the winter
that will burst into flame in the spring
and he sits upon a branch
and looks into my cabin window
wondering why i smile.

December 28

METAPHOR: Master Anglator?
ANGLATOR: Yes.

METAPHOR: The THING: Far, far upstream, where the spring churns up from the belly of the earth, there stands a tree. It draws its sustenance from the rich earth, rain, and through photosynthesis draws from the sun and air. The spring waters bubbling at its feet once fell as rain and settled into the earth, through layers and layers filtered until they reached the underground cavern from which pressure forced it back to the surface, percolating it to purity. Some of the waters mingle with the tree and some flow downstream, eventually to the ocean. But this tree . . . this tree . . . branches to unforeseeable directions yet still retains all that makes it a tree. And on the ground, in the tree, in the water – insecta fulfill their destinies. Some reproduce and some fall prey to the trout. And the trout move upstream and down at their specified times to spawn. But here . . . here . . . it all becomes so visible. I am a part yet apart from this and cannot help but alter it by my mere presence. I can only approach it on its own terms and yet in my own way. I choose my way. I choose the branching way.

ANGLATOR: Master Metaphor, indeed!

December 29

The wheel will turn
and i will die
and i know this
and accept it
as i hope you will

but i promise
that i will do all
within my power
to do it right

and by that
all i mean
is that i will try not
to die on your birthday
or christmas

or opening day
or any special day
that might pain you to remember

because if you are here
and i am gone
you still have a cycle to complete
and i hope to not jar that
with saddening memory
but rather to leave you with
remembrances of the whole thing
balanced

and i do not bid you adieu
prematurely
but offer my hopes to you
within the context
and remind you
that i care.

December 30

now –
      do you know?
– who stands by the river
– casting a line
– watching the flow
– taking it in
– searching
– learning understanding

do you know?
      – what it is
      – if it is worth doing
      – if it leads to an answer
      – if it has meaning
      – if it is good

       – if there is a reason to do it
do you know?

has this been worthwhile
       considering all the elements
       that went into it
has this brought any improvement or clarity
eh?

i cannot answer for you
i cannot presume to know your purpose
       or wish
i can only offer that it has brought me
       to where i needed to be
and no matter how trivial it looked
       to any other
it enveloped my being
       and i have done and been
what i should.

i speak for me –
       do i have my answers?
       did it enhance my being?
       was it worth the doing?

December 31

yes!